2.⁵⁰

Miracle at Square Top Mountain

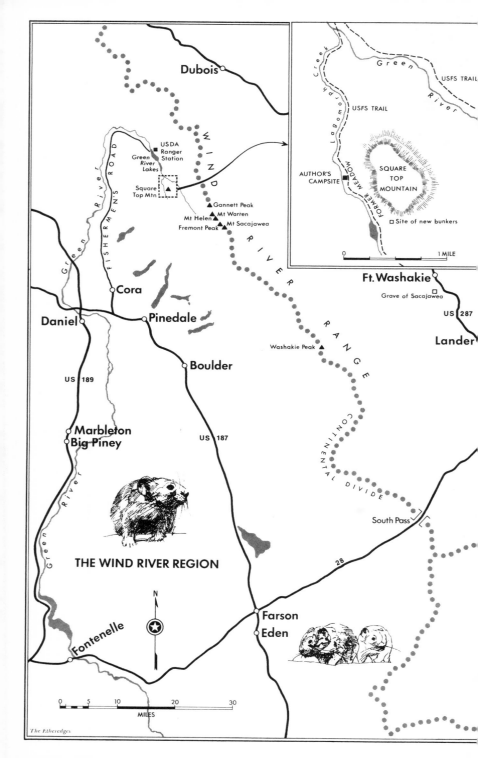

Dubois

WIND

USDA
Ranger
Station
Green
River
Lakes

Square
Top Mtn

▲ Gannett Peak
Mt Helen ▲▲
Fremont Peak ▲▲ Mt Sacajawea
Mt Warren

RIVER

RANGE

FISHERMEN'S ROAD

Green River

Cora

Daniel

Pinedale

Boulder

US 189

Washakie Peak ▲

CONTINENTAL

Marbleton
Big Piney

US 187

Green River

THE WIND RIVER REGION

N

Fontenelle

Farson
Eden

28

DIVIDE

South Pass

0   5   10   20   30
MILES

The Etheredges

Creek

Green

River

USFS TRAIL

Lagoom

USFS TRAIL

AUTHOR'S
CAMPSITE

FORMER   MEADOW

SQUARE
TOP
MOUNTAIN

□ Site of new bunkers

0   1 MILE

Ft. Washakie

Grave of Sacajawea   □

US 287

Lander

ALSO BY ROBERT FRANKLIN LESLIE

Read the Wild Water
High Trails West
The Bears and I
Wild Pets
Wild Burro Rescue
Wild Courage
In the Shadow of a Rainbow

Illustrated with drawings by John Schoenherr

Miracle at
Square Top Mountain

Robert Franklin Leslie

E. P. Dutton   New York

To
Wadsworth and Nancy Pohl
with deepest affection

Contents

Author's Note

According to legend, many aboriginal Americans expanded their tribal culture to include adoration of life forms. With adoration there developed a compulsion to communicate. Although early native people in other parts of the world achieved degrees of mental exchange between themselves and certain so-called lower animals—and thus began domestication—no record of communication among men and wild creatures approached the sophistication certain Amerind (American Indian) tribes developed.

Reception and understanding of wild animal messages—as well as frequently claimed communion with plants—became a conscientiously studied art, practiced by sachems, sagamores, shamans, medicine men, and witch doctors. Shamans carefully tested each acquired bit of knowledge before passing it along through esoteric ceremony to selected successors.

During childhood, I had heard my Cherokee father's old folks speak of *optical communication* between man and animals. Quite by accident and many years later, I undertook a serious investigation of that subject in deep wilderness with no pressures from without to interrupt the study. Under the scrutiny of Marcos Eagle Rock, a Wyoming Shoshone shaman, I lived in close proximity with a colony of Wind River Range pikas and a friendly yearling black bear, all of whom engaged in specific examples of interchanged messages.

In the 1870s Eagle Rock's parents had studied the same subject in far greater depth under the tutorship of Bird Woman, Sacajawea, heroine of the Lewis and Clark Expedition (1804–1806). At no time have I pretended that my endeavor embodied a purely scientific experiment; nevertheless, the story that follows is a strictly factual account of what took place. I have plainly labeled all personal feelings and observations; and although I tried to keep my diary notes free from exaggeration, I have purposely omitted many extraordinary, but nonetheless genuine, anecdotes that might appear overstated.

I should like to point out that my relationship with Eagle Rock at times suffered, for two reasons. First, I could not accept certain religious aspects he attributed to the communication experience, which he called *eye talk* or *eye language*. His *Earth Mother*, while worthy of respect because that was his honest belief, failed to supplant certain tenets instilled by my father's teaching. Second, in light of several tragic sequences, it became obvious that the Shoshone had deliberately withheld vital information I thought he should have imparted to me. Conflict developed between us because he believed I had meddled in the lives of wildlings beyond the terms of our original agreement. Marcos Eagle Rock had the beguiling habit of being right most of the time.

In order to protect the privacy of people still living in the region of Lander, Wyoming, the name "Howell" is fictitious.

ROBERT FRANKLIN LESLIE

The most beautiful thing we can experience is the mysterious. It is the source of all true art and science.

ALBERT EINSTEIN

Marcos Eagle Rock

Having concluded a biological research project in Canada somewhat sooner than expected, I was dawdling in leisurely fashion along the homeward route to California. On July 12, 1959, I swung the station wagon into the Shoshone Indian village of Fort Washakie, Wyoming.

As a youngster I had read every available anecdote about the Shoshone Bird Woman, the Amerind guide responsible for the success of the Lewis and Clark Expedition. I had followed her return route from the Columbia River to the Wind River Indian Reservation, where she devoted the rest of her life to tribal welfare in council with the illustrious Chief Washakie.

I stopped at a seedy little hillside cemetery two miles from Shoshone tribal headquarters. Kneeling on a path of sunbaked clay, I pulled dead weeds from Sacajawea's ne-

glected grave near the hilltop. Her two sons' headstones
lay one on each side of their famous mother's marker.

Weather-bleached plastic bouquets on rows of otherwise disregarded graves constituted a twentieth-century
abomination throughout the cemetery. An artificial comedy. Suddenly I became aware of an elderly Shoshone
gentleman towering above me. He had slunk up without a
sound. From beneath a wide-brimmed black stetson, his
eyes glowered like those of an infuriated eagle. Two thin
gray braids dangled from his temples and swung like
coiled cotton sash cords halfway down a faded blue denim
shirt he had not bothered to stuff into his jeans. At the sag
in a chain around his wrinkled neck hung a silver-
mounted adamant, establishing the presumption that the
weathered Shoshone held a tribal office of shaman. I
turned from the weeds and the artificial flowers to an
angry Amerind who was grumbling through gritting teeth.

"Why the hell are you desecrating Bird Woman's

grave?" He spoke in a dangerous monotone. His question hurled the weight of an outright challenge to my intrusion. "And I might respectfully ask the Shoshone why the hell you allow this great woman's grave to be defiled by a crop of low-down burweeds?" By the end of the question I was ashamed of myself for shouting.

"What you have uprooted, Mister, are *not* 'low-down burweeds!' Through these tough plants we know that Sacajawea's spirit still lives here. I hate these goddamned plastic flowers." His hand cut a swath across the sunparched cemetery. "Like the little two-by-twelve signs up and down the highway, nailed to telephone poles. 'Sacajawea Grave.' " He removed his hat and mopped perspiration from the sweatband with a faded red bandana. He wiped his neck and forehead. I stood up and did the same. "Not a dozen people a year give a damn where Sacajawea's grave is. And what brings *you* here, besides curiosity?" Mystical verve seemed to flash from the old gentleman's eyes. The smoldering July sun glared down as if trying to match Shoshone ardor.

We both sat down, backs against the shabby little headstone. In 1963 the DAR erected a more appropriate granite monument. I told the old shaman why I had come to visit the cemetery. He acted as if he disbelieved my answer to his question. We stoked our pipes from my tobacco pouch.

That meeting at Sacajawea's graveside on July 12, 1959, was destined to alter his life and mine.

"You know about Sacajawea, of course?"

"Naturally I know about Sacajawea." He spat and wiped the edges of his time-furrowed mouth. "My parents were young when Bird Woman taught them—before she died in eighteen eighty-four. I'm Shoshone. Marcos Eagle Rock. My mother called me Little Chief Speaker, because she heard a coney whistle when I was born up yonder in the Wind River Range. During juniper berry harvest. She

promised our Earth Mother that I'd always speak for
coneys. My father heard the Great Speaker say I would relate to coneys, just as he had done all his life. All Indians
relate to an animal *yek* [spirit helper]. Shoshones believe in
the immortal soul of every plant and animal."

Pikas or coneys, called Little Chief hares by Western
Amerinds, are small, rabbitlike mammals that inhabit
rocky, mountainous slopes between 8,000 and 14,000 feet
above sea level.

We shook hands. I introduced myself and explained
in greater detail why I had come to pay my respects at my
heroine's grave. As we puffed our pipes, I wondered if the
old gentleman weren't a bit shaky. "Speaker for coneys.
Spirits of dead coneys. *Yek.*" Perhaps the sticky July heat
had gotten to him. While he revealed several highlights of
his life history, I knew enough not to interrupt. Amerind
shamans and sagamores rarely gave lengthy speeches even
while passing tribal lore to a succeeding generation au-
thorized to receive it.

"My father was Tall Feather, a Cherokee," I said
when the first opening developed.

"My father was White Hare," Eagle Rock continued.
Ancestral pride shone from his wide-open expression. "All
his life he insisted the Little Chief hare—that's the
coney—was his ancient root. Some people call them whistling hares or rock hares. In the Bible there's a proverb that
says, 'The conies are but a feeble folk, yet make they their
houses in the rocks.' "

Eagle Rock spoke of his college days and of thirty
years behind a schoolteacher's desk somewhere in Montana. Despite this background, he had not been persuaded
that Agur's biblical coneys were hyraxes (ungulate mammals)—resembling slightly but in no way related to New
World or Asian coneys. The word *pika*, which originated
in Tungusic (Mongolian) dialect, is the correct term for the
species. *Never* coney—according to zoologists.

"A large colony of Little Chief hares—about thirty—hangs on up yonder in the Wind Rivers. Near the springhead of the Green River." He slowly pointed as if tracing the skyline twenty or thirty miles to the west: the Sacajawea cluster of 13,000-foot peaks. "Little Chiefs aren't rodents, you know. They're first cousins of rabbits and hares. Look just like a chinchilla without a tail."

"Yeah, zoologists call them *lagomorphs*. Not rodents."

Pikas, *Ochotona princeps*, inhabit western North America and certain parts of Asia at elevations within the hudsonian and alpine life zones; a distant relative lives at sea level in Washington and Oregon. The word *Ochotona* is Mongolian for "hare"; *princeps* is Latin for prince or "little chief." It was significant that pre-Columbian Shoshones called the pika *Little Chief hare*. Strange also that such a little-known animal had so many common names: Little Chief, rock rabbit, tailless hare, whistling hare, calling hare, starved rat, piping hare, and rock coney.

"They're smart, too. Real smart," Eagle Rock said between matches expended in futile attempts to keep his pipe lit. "They have sense enough to watch every sunset and sunrise. They won't bed down till afterglow. They whistle a special song at sunrise. Real smart. Since I retired from teaching ten years ago, I've spent more time in the mountains. I visited the Little Chiefs earlier this month. Square Top Mountain's where they live. They told me we'd have early winter this year. They asked me to help them with their harvest—till the middle of August or the first of September. They indicated frost about the twentieth of August. Winter in early September."

"They *told* you? *Asked* you to help them?" I didn't pretend to ignore the old man's hyperboles.

"Of course they *told* me. Not like I'm telling you here. Not with words, of course. But they told me all right. I've communicated with them all my life."

He paused, picked up an inchworm, and held it above

his head. Instantly a hermit thrush flew to his cupped palm, seized the worm, then returned to the roof of one of the two ancient board-and-batten privies that profaned the cemetery even more than the plastic flowers, much outdoing Sacajawea's headstone in visibility. A moment later a linnet landed on Eagle Rock's outstretched fingers and perched long enough to eat a dozen mustard seeds before returning to the cemetery's barbed wire fence. Obviously the old shaman got along with wildlife.

"The Little Chiefs told me through their eyes."

I had just witnessed confirmation of mental contact with two wild beings. The performance appeared to prove that the Amerind was not totally sentimentalizing. My interest persevered despite the sultry heat. Since boyhood, I had heard many accounts of Amerind communication with wildlings, so Marc's assertions came as no great shock. He may have detected my eagerness to know more about his experience.

"While I was up there," he continued after further delay with his pipe, "we listened together to the starlit nights."

"You and the pikas?" I asked, brow still raised.

"Yes. Dark of the moon. That's the only time you know what the stars *really* reveal. They warned of early frost, drought, and deep freeze. The Little Chiefs want me to help them bring in their winter hay before what we call black frost. They don't hibernate, you know. And they have to eat all winter from what they store in the summer. Their fodder has to be cut, cured, and stacked just like hay, at least forty pounds of dried material for each pika—about 500 man-hours of harvesting on the meadow and delivering to the bunkers on the talus. But I can't do it."

His voice subsided into a low metrical cadence like the legendary chants or half-whispered prayers that mystic medicine men intone—throaty echoes that charm instantly and galvanize the attention of all who listen. Quite often the old man's silent gestures divulged his meanings as directly and effectively as speech itself. With a flourish of both hands that symbolized futility, he explained what thwarted his helping the colony with its harvest.

"Because Little Chiefs neither migrate nor hibernate, they cut and spread their fodder to dry. Then they interlace it into ricks we call *garners*—about the size of a bushel basket—near their chambers, so they can eat close to home all winter. If a cold snap comes too soon, the frost rots any unripened fodder. If the air's too cold or damp, the sun won't toast the leaves and stems they want to cure. Hay won't keep if it goes untoasted. Funny thing. They sometimes prefer to cut it in cloudy weather. They know more about weather than we do."

He nibbled his lower lip with teeth surprisingly white for a man his age, relit his pipe, and dwelt at length with half-closed eyes on the towering mountains to the west of us.

"This colony lives at ten thousand feet. Most will starve before the deep snows of winter melt next June, unless . . ."

He shuttled his dark brown eyes back and forth between my face and the distant range. Age had in no way affected his vision or the strength of character that beamed when he focused his piercing gaze.

"Are they wild and hard for a stranger to approach? I've heard somewhere that coneys—or pikas—are among the most timid . . ."

"It's people that make animals wild. No human scent or sound or movement scares them unless they associate man with trouble. Fortunately, this new generation of Americans has begun to respect life."

"You say you're the Little Chief Speaker. So why the hell can't you help your Little Chiefs? Since they're under all that pressure. You're retired. What's to keep you from it?" I hadn't ruled out the possibility that the old shaman might be suffering some kind of confusion.

"My sister has no one to harvest her wheat and corn and beans. Husband died in June. Unfortunately, the human and pika harvests come at the same time. I have heart trouble. I came here to contact Sacajawea. Shoshones believe she intercedes when the cause is just."

Suddenly the strangest feeling prowled about my mind. A tingling sensation crept over me as if I were about to break out in a rash. The old man's stabbing gaze stood poised in ambush every time I turned my head and met his eyes. Through later events I would come to realize Eagle Rock exercised limited psychic leverage. I certainly changed my mind about his being confused. He waylaid me with an almost hypnotizing power behind that formidable stare.

"Would your Little Chiefs accept someone else— other than a Shoshone—to help them with their harvest? I'm a schoolteacher myself—in southern California. I don't have to be back on the job until late September."

"The Little Chief hares would accept help from anyone, provided such a person prove true friendship for them and genuine understanding, provided such a person work from sunrise to sunset for them till their harvest is in."

One further consideration occurred to me. "A number of other creatures—including grizzly bears, moose, and cougars, so I've been told—inhabit that rockery. What would I do about them? I don't carry weapons of any kind—only camping gear."

"That depends," he answered with his first smile that afternoon. "Depends upon how much you are willing to learn."

"What do you mean, Eagle Rock? Level with me, will you?"

"You Anglos are pursuers of shadows. And by the

way, before you make any rash decision, let me warn you that all Shoshones fancy the Little Chief hare. We don't stand for nonsense where a sacred belief is concerned. You have to learn to live with *all* life forms. Man has no animal enemies in the Wind River Range."

Although my father was an Amerind, Eagle Rock thought of me as an Anglo because I had inherited many of my Scottish mother's physical characteristics.

Notwithstanding the briefness of our acquaintance, I detected in Marcos Eagle Rock an imposing intelligence enhanced by academic education and honest, accurate feelings. His background was one of discernment, culture, appreciation, and respect for life—with a justified measure of intolerance and cynicism toward white men. I believed in him because suddenly I wanted to. Because he was believable. His teaching experience, study, and rural Amerind background genuinely qualified him to probe certain wildlife mysteries that were as vital to me as to him.

One distinctive quality especially persisted: there appeared to be not the slightest doubt concerning the genuineness of the old teacher's beliefs about pikas. More important, he was too endowed with Shoshone independence and principle to speak with forked tongue, too naked of veneer to speak other than truth. Despite almost eighty years of intense application to books and the Amerind's encyclopedia of nature, he was clearly a man motivated by an uncomplicated, basic incentive, a conviction that he stood for what was right regarding his Little Chiefs. Granted, he steeped his conversation in ancient, legendary beliefs, but the pride he cherished in his heritage bore the keen edge of reason. Even when he was angry Eagle Rock displayed the Shoshone refinement of built-in good manners. His carefully weighed statements celebrated well-honed symbols of the best Amerind intellect. In those few minutes he satisfied me that he wholeheartedly believed in the pikas' vital importance to both of us. Had Marcos

Eagle Rock chosen to live most of his days among his own people, rather than teaching school in Montana. I dare say they would have revered him as a mouthpiece of their deities. He believed emphatically that he possessed what it took to communicate with wild animals.

We both recognized almost simultaneously a common peg for mutual confidence. We both loved the memory of Sacajawea. We both loved wildlings. We were both small-town schoolteachers. We soon learned that we both held master's degrees in ecology. How novel in retrospect that by an accidental detour or act of fate a remarkable sequence of events had germinated in a tangle of countryside weeds on Sacajawea's grave!

For the next hour, Eagle Rock revealed that he had lived close to his Earth Mother, even during his schoolteaching years, that the principal ingredient of his mental well-being issued from a rugged—almost savage—intimacy with the outback wild, despite several recent bouts with heart disease. His eyes, like those of many animals I have known, reflected communion with the universal life force—a phenomenon easier to describe than to explain. His expression seemed to glow with untroubled belief in the Great Speaker, Gitche Manito: Indian equivalent of God.

In varying degrees, living close to the wild is a secret, primary delight that haunts everyone's heart. Perhaps for that reason, as much as my interest in optical communication, it had not been difficult for the old shaman to direct my thoughts toward the Wind Rivers.

Both in Canada and in the United States, Amerind relatives and friends at one time or another had revealed to me in confidence specific examples of communication with birds and mammals. Too often I had dismissed those curious proceedings as tribal legend—beautiful, but hollow-boned speculation like the fascinating yarns my father's old people used to spin. Since several dozen sophisticated men and women had often alluded to interspecific messages exchanged between the species through the eyes, I envisioned Square Top Mountain, a high point of the Jim Bridger Wilderness, as a laboratory where a deliberate experiment could be set up with a colony of wild animals that had no doubt experienced a degree of empathy with a human being. I had no special notion of proving anyone right or wrong. I simply didn't subscribe without reservation to beliefs and claims beyond the scope of my own experience with animals. I don't deny that my motivation at that moment encompassed little more than curiosity to see whether a person could indeed achieve intelligent mental performance with specific animals that had been somewhat pretrained for the endeavor. My experiences as a young man raising three bears in the wilderness of British Columbia stood me in good stead for the physical exposure. Eagle Rock agreed to teach me the essentials necessary for minimum "dialogue" not only with pikas but also with other freeborn animals I would likely meet in the Jim Bridger Wilderness.

"Shoshones think whites overstep their place in the grand scheme of life. Their religion teaches them to *conquer* nature rather than cooperate with it. Many whites violate animal trust—disregard animal dignity and humility. So each animal responds according to what he recognizes—often reacts one way toward a red man, another way toward a white man.

"You've no connection whatever with Little Chief hares, Bob. I doubt you've ever seen or heard one. So, what the hell can you offer thirty pikas that by now may have been subjected to target practice by an unthinking child? A public trail runs for three hundred yards near the talus where the colony lives."

His sunbaked facial wrinkles deepened when he smiled. Even before asking the question, he probably suspected that my answer would predicate my experience.

"Any bond between me and your Little Chiefs will be one of mutual trust," I began. "I'll see to it that each pika's pantry holds more than a single family can eat for one winter. Beyond that, I promise nothing." I ran down a brief outline of experiences I had had with animals—qualifications, if you will.

" 'The hay is carried, and the tender grass showeth itself,' " Marcos Eagle Rock quoted. " 'And the herbs of the mountains are gathered in.' A fragile harvest."

"I know the ways of the hills, Marc, if not the ways of your fragile Little Chiefs. I was raised in the hills—by an *Indian* father. And lived on my own for a long time in the British Columbia boonies."

"You'd be willing to help with their harvest—using what communication I show you to that end, disclaiming everything else?"

"What do you mean, 'disclaiming everything else?' "

"I mean you must not attempt to influence or encroach upon their lives or change anything up there."

"Hell no! Why should I?"

"When many people see an animal, they want either to kill it and eat it or tame it and pet it. Degradation of the wild!" He nickered separately each word of his admonishment. "Wildlings must remain their own problem solvers."

"I'll respect your pikas. You can count on that. But I believe each person develops his own empathy with animals—in his own way. I'll do what I can to learn a little eye talk. Beyond that, my friend, you can't stampede a man to swear on his word."

"All right. Before you go, you must hear Shoshone wisdom about coneys," he said, apparently satisfied with my terms. "We help them only in years of meadow failure, early frost, or infestation. Never protect them or interfere in any way that would cause them to become dependent or lose their wildness."

"Doesn't man's help during harvest encroach upon their lives? Doesn't that make them dependent upon man?"

"Not for a specific season, Bob, unless you overdo it. Some will die *because* of our help. More would die *without* our help. The important thing is that the *colony* or the *species* survives. Just don't get yourself emotionally involved. Is that clear?"

"That may be difficult for me, Marc. I've been involved all my life with wild animals. And every involvement has been one of genuine love and other emotions."

"I reckon I know what you mean," he said softly.

Rockslideland

Eagle Rock frowned threateningly as if he might withdraw me from the project when he saw me take down in shorthand a pocket notebook everything that he thought I should know about communicating with his pikas. He grunted disapproval every time I made any written record of our conversation. He accused me of collecting material for a newspaper article.

"Indian law recognizes the necessity of love in all nature," he resumed at last. "Life itself begins with love. Love is the inevitable goal of every living creature. Not wealth. Not security. But love. The *animal* manifestation is love. You'll find that true in pikaland . . . I often call it Rockslideland. Love the pikas by allowing them to remain as they are."

*   *   *

He talked until sundown. I had never heard an Amerind say as much. In that time he attempted to tell me everything he knew about Little Chiefs, although later I was to discover several outstanding omissions that I believed he should have mentioned.

Physically, the Little Chief has a thick body, eight to ten inches long. Weighs at most a pound—averages less. No tail. Face like a cottontail. Short ears, set way back on his head—broad, rounded, edged with white for high visibility. By wiggling his ears, he often transmits semaphore signals with complex meanings. All species have rabbitlike noses with long, silky whiskers sensitive to sound, smell, and feeling. Except when calling or eating, they clench their teeth.

"Pika color blends with the rocks where they live. Brownish beige is commonest. Some get almost black if they live in basalt or lava. Their bellies vary from cinnamon to buffy white. Even among light yellow ones there is some slaty black hair. Makes them look translucent—and so, another name: rock ghost.

"The Little Chief walks, crawls, and scurries with a rolling gait. Even canters like a mustang. Never hops like a rabbit. He grows long hair on the soles of his feet, but not on the toe pads. Can't lose footing when he leaps from boulder to boulder. Sometimes broad jumps fourteen feet. Leaps with all fours, not like a rabbit or a squirrel or a cat. In a hurry, he bounces down a talus like a tennis ball dropping down a flight of stairs. Hairy front paws also serve as a washrag for his face, neck, and ears. He bathes just like a cat except when he hankers for an overall soaking come rain or a trip to the creek.

"His hind legs are a little longer than the front. Wears thick-haired pantaloons to hide his legs completely except when he jumps. Almost never drinks water. Gets his moisture from dew or plant juices.

"Males and females look exactly alike. Their eyes protrude like a squirrel's—dark brown, polished zircon. I've seen them stare for ten minutes into the wind without blinking.

"Pikas rarely practice self-defense. But sometimes they gang up on a weasel or a snake. Claws unfit for digging or fighting. Mouth and teeth too small to bite most enemies. They can't goose it fast enough to outrun predator birds.

"One species gets by in the Gobi Desert with burrows, but our pikas don't dig out true burrows, warrens, or bunkers. They line their nests in natural corridors, hollows, and chambers under Rockslideland boulders.

"They sneak out at night to investigate disturbances in their 'village.' While they're out, they sing—maybe to the stars, maybe to the wind. They plod day and night under the harvest moon, but otherwise they are daytime animals. They crawl to the crests of boulders any time for exposure to wind or rain. They enjoy bucking a gale so the wind can comb their fur against the grain. You'll see them clinging to rocks in the heaviest rainstorms. They're tough!

"The Little Chief climbs dwarf aspens, junipers, alders, and chokecherries for fruit, shoots, and leaves. Eats thistles, wild rose stems, prickly geums, and all sorts of grasses. Strictly herbivorous. No flesh. Never gets fat even during summer abundance. But you understand there is no true summer up there.

"Males mate for life, normally with one female. Sometimes two. One to four offspring are born in May and weaned six weeks later. The young rarely show above the passageways until early July. You never see a *little* coney unless the weasel prowls. Mothers drill their broods to outrun certain predators on the open talus, but the youngsters stick close to their parents for the first six months. Then they associate as apprentices with older unmated ones who train them in more subtle aspects of survival.

"Little Chiefs practice ventriloquism. Confuses their enemies. The body jerks forward and upward each time a coney throws his voice. They always sound as if they were farther away than they really are.

"If you're willing to hold by the truth, I'll send you to Rockslideland, to my brothers and sisters, the Little Chief hares. But remember above all else the ultimate doctrine that all wildlings *must* remain wild animals."

His eyes dissected me.

"Why did you leave your people for so long, Marc?" I asked, more point-blank than I had intended.

He smiled. "As a farmer, I couldn't grow thistles. Even less luck as a medicine man; my patients all died. After my young wife died, I went to college. Took a temporary teaching job in Montana. Stayed thirty years. Under another name, of course—and a crew cut—for business reasons in those days. Never remarried."

"I know exactly what you mean. Let's go. I'll drive you home. You can mark Square Top Mountain on the road map. I'll give your harvest a try."

"You can locate the colony without any sweat," he said. "Take the fishermen's road from Cora to the lower Green River Lake. From there you hike. Take the trail to the right. Follow Porcupine Creek Trail signs as if you were going to Twin Lakes. Just after you pass the big marsh above the upper Green River Lake, hit the only trail to Square Top Mountain's northwest talus. And that's it."

As we walked down the hill, he picked up chewing gum wrappers, cigarette butts, and film cartons carelessly tossed among the graves. "Odd how people will litter a cemetery nowadays," he said as he dropped the trash into a rusty oil drum at the gate.

"How do I recognize Square Top Mountain?"

"It's the only mountain that rises directly behind upper Green River Lake. More of a round monolith than a mountain. Stands by itself, half a mile high, half a mile thick. Dominates the whole scene. Looks like a big tree stump left by Paul Bunyan. You'll see a talus slope of loose boulders piled up against the northwest wall of the mountain. That's Rockslideland. To the Little Chiefs, it's home. At the foot of the talus you'll cross a meadow. Extends all the way across the canyon to a timberline forest of lodgepole pines. From that meadow the coneys harvest their winter silage. You can bed down at my campsite in the lodgepoles near the creek. You'll meet a yearling black bear that hangs around those parts. He's an orphan, a clown, and a nuisance. Scare him away."

As I drove the old gentleman to his sister's farm near Lander, he assured me that I would see more of him later. During the twenty-five-mile trip, he expanded on the miracle of optical communication, illustrating from his own experiences how he distinguished between communication and simple vision. "For example," he said, "a coney emerging from a den surveys the immediate surroundings for any kind of danger. Once satisfied concerning family safety, he may look for food, weather information, amusement, relaxation, or contest. Communication begins when a family member follows the first pika and seeks similar information. Without external body signals, a flashing glance may reveal the basic outline of what a relative may expect to find—danger or security. As a rule, an intelligent message comes from muscular, vocal, and scent devices as well as optical signals; but the optical cue dominates all others. The eyes of intelligent animals *receive* factual information and *reflect* attitudes. Getting the receiver's attention is the first requirement before a message can be delivered.

"The basic sensations of all animals are love, ambition, hate, anger, fear, pride, passion, grief, joy, pain, aggression, worry, doubt, hunger, and well-being," he continued. "The eye broadcasts unmistakably each impression—with degree and quality. It all boils down to instantaneous recognition of a specific feeling. Ordinarily, you can say a lot through your eyes. In fact, certain attitudes that can't be expressed with words can be communicated perfectly through the eyes.

"Tall Feather often said, 'The eye questions and answers without an uttered sound.' He believed that every animal studies and estimates our intentions through what it sees in our eyes, even at a distance. I've heard him say, 'Sight with insight probes the hidden soul.' "

Marcos Eagle Rock carried the principle a step further. "The eyes are the front door of the brain, the Earth Mother's most precious gift. In your eyes, my friend, not your tongue, Sacajawea's spirit placed an answer to the question I was about to ask her when I saw you desecrating her grave!"

"Marc, you speak like my father," I said, unable to suppress a grin. "Your silver linings are too damn big for your clouds!"

He laughed. "A defect of *inner* vision." As we shook hands at the farm, the shaman said, "If my sister's harvest goes well, I'll hike to Rockslideland from the village of Dubois, some fifteen miles to the northeast. Before frost. To see how you are getting along with the Little Chief hares. I'll borrow a horse if any chest pains crop up."

I spent the night in Lander.

By nine o'clock the next morning I had covered the 145 miles between Lander and the settlement of Cora, some twenty miles southwest of the Green River lakes. At Cora's general store I stocked the station wagon with supplies to last six weeks: my own food, a small sickle and sharpening stone, guinea pig pellets, hamster treats, and granola with which to purchase the pika colony's confidence. I bounced along the fishermen's primitive road above the frothing Green River. After creeping through miles of massive sage-covered highlands, the rocky, deep-rutted route snaked into a mixed conifer and aspen forest. Quite suddenly the rough byway dead-ended in a cul-de-sac of the Wind River Range. At a small campground I parked my car. The blue violet Green River Lake's two-mile length reflected a backdrop of glacier-corniced peaks, all more than 13,000 feet above sea level. Gannet, Fremont, Downs, Warren, Helen, Sacajawea, and many more—Wyoming's saw-toothed horizon of the Continental Divide. As the most outstanding nearby landmark, however, Square Top Mountain dominated every physical feature of the range.

Like a gigantic black mesa from the bottom of a V between the Saltlick Range to the west and the 13,000-foot Continental Divide to the east, Square Top rises 11,679 feet above sea level. The canyon of the infant Green River along the east face fans out into a flat saucerlike basin that holds both Green River lakes immediately north of the talus Eagle Rock called Rockslideland. The broad-floored canyon of Porcupine Creek and another stream extends westward toward the Saltlick watershed. South of Square Top Mountain, the Wind River Range peaks dominate every mile of the horizon for as far as the human eye can see. Those who have seen the movie *Close Encounters of the Third Kind* will have a vivid impression of Square Top Mountain scenery, for the picture was filmed on location there years after my sojourn.

Of my long and roundabout journey, there remained but five or ten miles of Bridger National Forest trail to Eagle Rock's pikas. At first glance an inexperienced flatlander would have sworn that a good hiker could stomp out that trek to the talus in about three hours. After boxing half the supplies in the station wagon for later pickup, I stuffed the other half into the rucksack along with camping gear.

Slowly and laboriously, I skirmished along the cobble-strewn path around the lake's western shoreline. Trail washouts and strained breathing at that altitude exacted an hour of exasperating labor merely to reach the end of the first lake. No hint of autumn sharpened the atmosphere or mitigated the sun's fiery fist. Maybe the Amerind and his pikas had misguessed about early winter.

After contemplating a grouchy 1,500-pound bull moose that was slopping around in the upper Green River Lake and broadcasting a surly optical message that I was *not* welcome, and after passing with due respect the tracks a 600-pound grizzly bear had imprinted on a muddy section of the trail, I congratulated myself that the target animal in this experiment weighed at most one pound.

At length I left the Porcupine Creek Trail and puffed onto the unmarked Forest Service path that served local game up and down the Green River watershed. The route rose steeply at first, then terminated in a small valley with forest and noisy creek on one side and a flowering meadow on the other. Beyond the meadow and directly across from the forest, time and violent weather had piled a fifty-five-degree slope of dark reddish black boulders halfway up the cliff of the overwhelming Square Top Mountain. That quarter-mile slope was a talus.

Great Sun on high! I suddenly realized that talus was Rockslideland! Dreaming along the spectacular route, I had come upon the site so suddenly that I was completely unprepared for its tremendous impact. But where the hell were the pikas?

Relieved to unshoulder the heavy pack, I plopped onto a boulder at the end of the meadow in order to regain breath and tell myself that I had indeed arrived. Mopping a flood of perspiration from my face, I began to assess the neighborhood. No wild faces popped out into the open with stared "messages," although I had an itchy feeling that I was a target of scrutiny from all sides. Before skirting the grassy glade and prowling into a thin stand of inhospitable tamarack (lodgepole pine) to set up camp for six weeks, I procrastinated in order further to savor the scenic magnificence.

A distracting updraft, soughing over the talus slope, delivered an invigorating tang of resin, sage, and beemint from canyons below. Big puffy cumuli moved in and milled around storm-whittled peaks to the east and southeast. The Wind River Mountains bore the autograph of antiquity and at the same time the freshness of constant renewal. At that moment the Green River country looked like an excellent realm in which to bask in the Amerind way—an all-real place where drawn-out abstracts counted for less than substance of the moment.

Reshouldering the clumsy pack, I crossed the meadow without stomping the faces of alpine coreopsis and established camp at Eagle Rock's fire pit. He had located this campsite directly across the meadow from the talus and sixty feet inside the haughty forest near a creek with no name. As the stream tumbled down its narrow channel, the water simulated the swishing sound of a running woman in a long taffeta evening gown, whispering over and over the word "lagomorph, lagomorph, lagomorph!" Without knowing why, I continued to expect a reception committee of pikas. Where were they? Had some unknown disaster wiped them out? Chattering and sassing chipmunks skittered about in abundance. A Franklin's grouse, tinkering with eternity, "asked" for some peanuts I was about to munch, but she refused to eat them until I washed off the salt. If that represented a fortuitous example of communication, I could understand why Eagle Rock had camped there. Other people had used the site, but had left little evidence of a lengthy stay. A cottontail rabbit and a large varying hare scampered to the anonymous stream to drink. Rabbits, hares, pikas. All lagomorphs. The brook seemed to cry out for the name Lagomorph Creek.

Shoshones gave daytime as well as nighttime names

to almost everything. By day the Wind River Range went by Cragrockland; by night, The Wall Below Heaven. Before sunset, trees were Forest Mothers; after dark they became Dream Speakers. Juniper made up the stunted alpine forest above 10,000 feet, called Berry Bush while Amerinds could still see to pick the fruit; at night, Whispering Shadows. Because Shoshones still considered the mountains tribal property, I would have to consult with Eagle Rock or a reservation council before seriously christening the unnamed stream Lagomorph Creek. After all, I was an outsider and perhaps the Amerinds had long ago given the brook a more appropriate name.

Sunshine teased the brooding forest shadows every time thick clouds opened a peephole around the jagged western summits and allowed vibrant yellow spotlights to caper into the somber aisles. During the final hour before sunset, however, the puffball clouds maneuvered into open sky; so I located and memorized the faces of prominent peaks authenticated on a topo map.

Because of ample space between the trees, Eagle Rock's campsite also functioned as a splendid lookout for scrutiny of the talus across the meadow. Erosion from the perpendicular cliffs of Square Top Mountain had stacked the disorderly slope with boulders. The talus was as steep as gravity permitted. I might have labeled it a monotonous landscape; indeed, a study of the map's vegetation lines had forewarned me that treeline canyons and valleys in the high country would reflect austerity—downright baldness.

While sitting on an observation boulder near camp— a boulder I quickly called the "armchair" rock because of its shape and function—and while scanning with binoculars, I watched the hunting techniques of a weasel, a pair of gray foxes, and a red-tailed hawk as they shuttled back and forth across the huge talus Eagle Rock called Rockslideland. If any pika still existed in the face of such formidable enemies, it was no thanks to the Earth Mother who had

provided them with barest minimum protection and nothing to fight with.

Eagle Rock's moth-eaten bear attested to the poverty
of the region by racing toward camp the moment he

smelled the supper I had begun to prepare. He was small for a yearling, not more than 150 pounds. His pelt was dark brown, rather than the black typical of his species when mature. The scrawny varmit ricocheted through the forest, stumbled—even hurtled against a tree and bellowed with a bruised nose—as he circled the man-smell, more intent upon sizing up the two-legged newcomer than upon watching where he was running. His skittish behavior betrayed an expectation of stones and invectives. When I walked to the armchair rock, deposited a graham cracker, and returned to the fire pit, the tattered bruin slowed down to a fast, circling walk, sniffed the air, charged up to the cracker, grabbed it, and clawed his way toward open meadow as if I were hot on his tail.

The slivery moon of July 13 had dropped behind the western crests before the bear inched slowly back toward camp. The honey-sweet taste of graham cracker lingered in his mouth and taunted his imagination. More important, as far as the bear was concerned, I surmised, was the memory that no measure of eviction had been taken against his hide. After braking to analyze samples of air, he tiptoed carefully to the same boulder and seized a second cracker. He gulped it quickly, then stood by at a short distance further to test the possibility of sticks and stones. Slowly I held up a third graham cracker.

Still suspicious, the young bear crept cautiously into camp, stopping every fourth or fifth step to sniff, growl, and listen. He invested more confidence in his senses of smell and hearing than in sight. But hunger and perhaps an overwhelming curiosity finally overcame his instinctive fear of whatever unpleasant experiences he may have absorbed while raiding fishermen's camps or strong-arming his competing neighbors. At length he threw all caution to the wind, reared, walked swiftly on his hind paws to where I stood, and stretched his neck almost to the point of losing balance when he took a third cracker from my hand. I rewarded him for his confidence with a fourth, fifth, and sixth as he stood there on his hind legs, forepaws outstretched in fighting stance—just in case I had a trick up my sleeve.

The threat of gusty canyon wind increased as the clouds moved west. The yearling and I sat down and locked eyeballs, studied the other's changing features rather than movements. Slowly we became more comfortable, each in a foreign presence. At length I began to experience the feeling of having made a friend; and by the firm composition of his facial expressions, I assumed the bear felt the same way. Thus, I became one small degree further convinced that a mysterious potential existed for serious communication through the eyes. Other animals were to prove snootier to woo and win as associates.

The bear's friendly visit seemed to transform the austere Cragrockland into a little more accessible wilderness, although his presence interfered at that time with my growing curiosity about the pikas and their inexplicable absence. Beyond the arbitrary forest limits—even beyond Square Top Mountain—across shintangle heaths, flowering meadows, and catchbasin lakes, a tremendous amphitheater sprawled its terraces beneath a moody sky—a colosseum where wild gladiators no doubt enacted deadly dramas within its hard arena.

Square Top looked its part: a severe mountain, with 1,700-foot perpendicular cliffs on three sides whose fissures in every contour belied its monolithic appearance when viewed from Green River Canyon. Droppings from those cliffs—everything from cabin-sized boulders to pebbles—clung precariously at the foot of one vertical granite crag. That slope was Rockslideland. Crevices, cul-de-sacs, chinks, corridors, and tunnels formed a honeycomb of air spaces—inner chambers in which labyrinths the frugal pika colonies over the centuries had built up small amounts of soil that glued the boulders in place. Most rocks had settled into more or less stable permanence, holding firm when blocks weighing several tons plunged from the overpowering crags and catapulted down the slopes—chunks that heat, ice, lightning, and earth tremors chiseled from Square Top's ancient wall. In sandstone strata the wind still gnawed fossil dinosaur bones.

When massive erosion spewed an unusual volume of boulders—in spite of the cementing effect of accumulated soil, sand, and organic dust—keystones at the foot of the talus sometimes slipped, precipitating avalanches that not only wiped out pika, marmot, chipmunk, and ground squirrel populations but also encroached upon the pro-

ductive acreage of neighboring meadows. Excessive overburden—cascading tonnage of rock, ice, snow, and rain—
could flip a cornerstone into space like a tiddlywink; the
resulting landslide gashed long gulches into the affected
talus, and it required thousands of years for Square Top to
refill them with chippings from the cliff.

As twilight delicately dimmed the bridge between day
and night on that first evening at the campsite, a warm
norther from the not-too-distant Tetons and a seering
souther from the nearby Red Desert Basin collided head-
on below the Square Top escarpments. From all appear-
ances, the two cyclonic air currents chose their battle-
ground along the Rockslideland inhabited, according to
Eagle Rock, by the pikas. To me it was just another windstorm; to the Little Chiefs it must have been a life-or-death
matter. Charging and howling, the untempered gusts
slashed hoarsely at the fluted columns above the slope
with sufficient din and fury to make animal ears ring and
hearts quail. This was no ordinary evening updraft from
the warm canyons below. Gossipy waterfowl on the
lakes—unwilling to surrender the calm of summer dusk to
the tempest—honked their displeasure. At top speed the
yearling bear scudded into denser forest downstream
where Lagomorph and Porcupine creeks joined.

Where could the pikas find refuge in such a twister?
As Eagle Rock had predicted, the Little Chiefs
emerged from subterranean bunkers and sang as if confe-
derating in the battle cries of the Cyclops. It was my first
assurance that the colony really existed. I stepped to the
edge of the forest and listened. Well-being seemed to
reign throughout Rockslideland, while elsewhere every
last wildling scrambled for deepest shelter. Between the
drony blasts, pika voices drifted down with flutelike quality. Even with binoculars, however, I was still unable to locate them; but in theory at least, I shared one oddball

pleasure with them: We both enjoyed the wind's every mood. Creekside aspens clapped their leaves vigorously as if applauding throughout the roily tempest. Thinking about supper, I returned to Eagle Rock's fire pit.

At 10,000 feet above sea level, an alpenglow of twilight burst with dramatic suddenness across the windswept range. Again I rushed from the forest campsite to the meadow in order fully to observe a brief return of daylight as the overcast cleared. The pikas relayed sharp cries of "eenk!" across the talus that rose halfway up Square Top Mountain. Through binoculars I saw twenty puffs of dark bluish gray fur appear one at a time along the sharpest ridges of widely scattered Volkswagen-sized boulders. They didn't move. But they were there. They had indeed emerged from their dens. Twenty pairs of obsidianlike eyes focused upon me without the slightest observable body movement, even when they "eenked" or when the wind twisted, pulled, and whipped their long, chinchilla-like fur. To get their reaction, I walked slowly to the upper end of the meadow. Still they didn't move, but their eyes followed me. Wherever I went, there was no escape from their fixed gaze, like that of an art-gallery portrait.

As dusk enveloped the Wind Rivers, the pikas extended their "eenks" to soft, warbled tremolos, barely audible above the wind—as obviously an animal song as I had ever heard. Not a cry. Not an alarm. A song. The wind was no stranger here. They were children of the wind. Other animals fled in terror, but the pikas came out and sang in the wind, perhaps because storm time was their only uninterrupted interval of security.

On that blustery evening I made up my mind to know the Little Chiefs to the greatest possible depth consistent with my agreement with Eagle Rock.

Many times in the weeks to come I was to notice that the stars pulsated more rapidly on windy nights like this because dust-laden air currents and jet streams, interlacing from opposite quarters, accelerated the motion of tiny particles in the upper atmosphere to produce more shimmering reflections. But on such nights I realized that forest fire danger was acute, so I made it a practice to pour water on the campfire and eat a cold supper. Yielding thus to momentary conditions, I often gained more time to lie on the sleeping bag and reflect upon the sparkling, blue black front porch of heaven.

Like ghostly tumbleweeds reeling across the sky, the last clouds wheeled over the eastern horizon, rolled away by the gale. The tumult gradually subsided. Shortly after the final gusts had charged beyond the Continental Divide, a few cloud streamers escaped and crept back as if trying to hide among the crestline peaks—up where glacier-packed ravines fountainheaded a dangerous flash flood each time hot gales from the Red Desert blasted over the northern slopes and released meltwater.

Soon after midnight the feeble calls from the pikas and other creatures—even the gossipy buzzes of tamarack needles and the kid-gloved clapping of aspens—ceased. The wilderness slept, but the brooklike Lagomorph Creek kept up a chattering semitone—a monotonously happy tune—as it purled over its stony bed.

As if they had not spent half the night fluting enthusiastic accompaniment to the windstorm, the pikas emerged from their grottoes at dawn the next day, July 14, and whistled as an energetic chorus. The caprock above the talus reflected an antique, garnet red patina in the early light, a reminder perhaps that the canyon indeed boasted hoary age, despite its youthful sounds. A morning downdraft radiated the delicious breath of ripe juniper berries from an upper heath where cedar waxwings sang as they crunched the fragrant fruit. A hermit thrush's reedy notes inspired melodious tunes from dipper ouzels at streamside. Swallows flew erratic missions into the few remain-

ing gnat and mosquito swarms. The itinerant yearling
bear, little more than a yawning shadow at sunrise, waddled cautiously onto the meadow and slurped yellow
wood slugs—evidence of a nonfastidious appetite. Although pikas trilled the canyon's loudest morning tunes,
they often yielded the stage to superior songsmiths that
warbled squatters' rights when competitors appeared.

In the stark light of sunrise, the Wind River Range
struck me as a land of contrasts—stone-rimmed, disfig-
ured, devilishly inhospitable, yet at the same time over-
flowing with song. When I went to the brook for water, the
startling contrasts of the orderly floored forest were also
emphasized when I saw that delicately tinted columbines
dripped with blood from a freshly slain fawn. A silent kill
on a noisy night.

After dried prunes, cold cereal, and reconstituted
milk, I could hardly wait to sickle an enormous armful of
herbs on the meadow and climb the talus so the gaping
pikas could see me carry the harvest offering. Somehow I
had acquired the naive notion that such an exhibition
would prove my collaboration in their harvest. From
gleaning to delivery entailed a devastating slog, an extended communion with bigness compounded by strange-
ness and harshness, a sample break-in, as it were, to what I
might expect in the weeks to come, provided the pikas accepted me—provided I learned to communicate with them
to some reasonable degree.

During the ascent of that flinty talus, I frequently
miscalculated footing, slipped, and sprawled over one jagged boulder after another. The black ramparts reflected
heat, hardness, and hostility. My boots were the wrong
kind for rock climbing. I should have bound my sheath of
forage onto a pack frame to free my hands so desperately
needed from boulder to boulder. I should have worn
gloves. The whole fiasco was a comedy of errors. Not one
pika emerged from the bunkers. They were probably

mourning the destruction of their meadow and quailing at the noisy monster flopping about their homeland.

Reaching the topmost rock next to Square Top's imposing cliff a quarter mile above the meadow, I groped for a handhold with paroxysms of uncertainty. Trousers torn, knees barked, shirt ripped, elbows skinned, hands cut and bleeding, I was a mess. Thank God nobody saw me! If the pikas peeked, they kept it a secret. My bundle of fodder had dwindled along the way; in fact, at the huge platform-like toprock, hardly enough dandelions remained to fill a bud vase.

The Pikas and Their Homeland

While regaining composure on that high talus platform, I pondered on the mystery of paradoxical violence and tenderness in the world of nature. Mystery often attached itself where contrasting spurts of violence and tenderness associated in paradox at the same wellhead. Mystery probably spawned deep-rooted Amerind beliefs in Earth Mother, Gitche Manito, and the Sun God.

A gentle down-canyon breeze that lifted a single grain of pollen from buttercup stamen to stigma exploded suddenly and swept a planing eagle to its death against a Square Top cliff. From what I learned on that first climb the talus appeared so dreadful with its exposure to climatic vicissitudes, falling boulders, fragile footing, and openness to carnivore attack that no animal with any possibility of survival elsewhere had ever been tempted to preempt a foothold on pika terrain. The very nature of the scree made animal movement slow and hazardous. Other than pikas, marmots, and chipmunks, not even the destitute sought refuge beneath a cliff that was still undergoing geological genesis; each falling chunk in conjunction with desiccating gales and avalanches rumbled a perpetual undertone of disaster. Every day saw the fall of rocks onto the talus; boulders on the slope shifted or rolled under the impact.

Throughout the Green River region, peril tempered most components of everyday life. The degree of danger varied in proportion as the circumference of an animal's forage range expanded. Nevertheless, personal hazard remained vague and subjective, depending less upon what was *apt* to happen than upon what *did* happen. Unpredictable danger crouched most of the time behind the violent or unstable forces of nature.

My platform boulder overviewed meadow, forest, lakes, peaks, and the canyon of the Green River. In times past, bulk detritus on both sides of the scree had cascaded toward the meadow, leaving deep gullies in the slope. Then for centuries erosion had toiled to refill every gaping gulch. A few gnarled lodgepoles on the slope barely withstood starvation. From that huge flat rock you could read the geological history of the range. You could contemplate all the wildlings that stared from safe distances.

I sensed elation in the granite spectra of umber and sienna, in the gorges of misty blue haze, in the sotto voce singsong of a babbly stream. Gradually I came to realize that every composition in the final analysis displayed its own boundless beauty of depth and color. The timeless severity of vermilion cliffs lost every aspect of silence and inflexibility when that hardness echoed the night bird's song. For lyric soliloquy and living color, you'd never surpass the variety in an evening chickadee's melody or the bright flare of scarlet tanager wings that lighted for a second or two a somber shadow among frugal tamaracks.

Monotony could never apply to a lightning thrust momentarily framed within a rainbow's delicate arch.

The herbland meadow below bristled with industry as small mammals, birds, and the doe with her remaining fawn searched for a meal of the moment, seemingly regardless of any signs foreshadowing early scarcity of pasture. Only the pikas harvested with an eye on winter.

It was not yet 8:00 A.M. A silver fox flushed a pika and chased him into a narrows between two boulders less than twenty feet away from where I was sitting. When the carnivore saw himself outmaneuvered, his ragged bark ruptured the morning silence. The result of a spontaneous flash of anger, reflex, or whatever, I jumped from my perch and hurled a golf-ball-sized stone that glanced ineffectually from the fox's shoulder. Glaring through squinting eyes, the surly beast swished his brush, stiffened his stance, and raised his hackles. Realizing the stone had come from my hand, he snarled and padded slowly across the talus, refusing me the satisfaction of believing I had frightened him into running away.

More than a dozen pikas, hunkering in concealed crevices, witnessed my rash deed. Their whistles clearly indicated alarm that I might throw the next stone at one of them. It seemed to me a surprisingly long time before they withdrew their stony stares and crawled into their bunkers among the rocks.

I decided to devote a week to observations in the mountain community. I had to get acquainted with its unbending regimen of austerity. There remained the possibility that my help—if indeed help was really needed—might annul vital instincts and interfere destructively with inborn patterns of behavior that had done an excellent job of perpetuating the pika species for eons.

Trying to turn the clear light of reality on my rosy vision, I realized almost at once that if I hoped to make the most of the adventure, my views must be somewhat modified. Whatever my personal feelings, I must steel myself against the anonymity and oblivion to which every natural creature was heir. This was a raw land of fast, deadly carnivores on the prowl for raw meat. The pika was considered a prey species during every season. That first trip to the top of the talus produced a resolution to remain as emotionally uninvolved as possible regardless of what might happen.

Although we marvel at nature's successes and esteem her miracles, we rarely question her capricious side. From the day of the first pulse of life on this planet, she has operated exclusively by accident, never by blueprint. She has always been fallible—glutted with mistakes. From primordial ooze to passenger pigeon, virtually everything she has learned has emerged through mistakes—trial and error. Her lightning fires have leveled her forests, incinerated her babies, eroded her soil, and polluted her waters—four whopping boners in one act, by human standards. She crowned man the mental king of beasts, but neglected to endow him with the regal responsibility to govern his own habitat.

As Tall Feather's son, my previous experiences with man and nature had been extensive and varied, but my knowledge of pikas went little further than recognition of distant whistles and a few quick glimpses through binoculars. I wondered whether Eagle Rock's Earth Mother would allow the colony to examine my "credentials" for being there. During that week between July 14 and 21, the pikas appeared to scorn my presence.

Honestly and truly confessed, I had reached a hasty decision to assist with the harvest because of one Amerind's contagious concern that early frost might devastate the Little Chiefs' winter food supply and thus jeopardize their survival. Beyond curiosity about optical communication, I foresaw no invincible dedication to the colony per se. I had the time; the cost of the project was negligible. With the slightest excuse, my country-bred feet have always shuffled toward any mountain wilderness; therefore, the undertaking presupposed lazy visions—three or four weeks of undisturbed backwoods reverie. To be aboveboard, I had set no tangible sights on an all-out pursuit of knowledge even should the venture reveal new phenomena.

Two aspects of the undertaking, however, fired increasing enthusiasm. First, after that initial climb, satisfaction in the sheer physical accomplishment might result in something I could be proud of; and second, there existed almost no available data concerning the pika way of life. As an ecologist, I suspected that about ninety-nine percent of the world's population had never heard of a pika; therefore, upon leaving the canyonland in August, I stood to contribute new information—hopefully a short paper on that so-called communication with an unknown species.

Beyond these motives, admittedly thin and shaky, I approached Eagle Rock's pikas with fragmentary drive and no devotion. My attitude bordered upon the grotesque in supposing that these little lagomorphs would accept a human stranger who began by spying into their privacy through binoculars, by attempting to buy their friendship with guinea pig pellets, hamster treats, and granola.

A number of possibilities strayed into my head. Suppose the pikas moved to another hillside when they saw their neighborhood profaned with armloads of weeds they had not ordered. At best I could expect a role of tolerance rather than acceptance, even though Eagle Rock had predicted the colonists would react as receptively as I did. In addition to a strong probability of rejection, the work itself already threatened to overwhelm me. That first attempt to carry one load of herbs up the treacherous slope had seriously eroded my will to continue. Heavy frost, I told myself, might dismantle the meadow earlier than August 15. Early frost might not occur at all. My presence might disrupt animal life other than pikakind—although at first there didn't appear to be much to disrupt at 10,000 feet above sea level.

Consequently, I could not pretend during that week of adjustment that my original decision to carry fodder for the pikas were more than a rash, momentary whim—an excuse to sojourn in the magnificent Wind River Range. Nevertheless, although superficial and hazy incentives may have clouded my first several days, a deluge of events subsequent to my stoning that fox resulted in an abundance of crystal-clear motives for staying there far longer than I had planned.

Meanwhile the pikas came and went—through the binoculars. Hugging knife-edged boulders and staring blankly, they simply scorned seven loads of fodder, delivered at painful cost to their front porches—an extravagant hostility, it seemed, in light of my potential for hauling in one day more provender than the entire colony could gather in a week. Concurring with Eagle Rock, I certainly wanted no taming that might despoil any cover of wildness; but for practical purposes, somehow I expected at least token cooperation. Whenever I stalked within twenty feet, they shrieked and scooted into their bunkers as if Satan himself were on the prowl.

In breathy midday heat on July 15, the little fools scampered en masse to the meadow where they glutted themselves on thistle blossoms, canes of spiny eglantine, and buckthorn, disregarding a plethora of succulent, nectar-laden lucerne, honey-sweet fiddlenecks, and juicy ripe strawberries. A simpleton could have recognized that Rockslideland presented unlimited opportunity in which to develop personal toughness; but at that time I winced in an effort to comprehend a dietary *choice* of thorns. Was it possible that such stupid beasts had indeed communicated with a human being?

Suddenly a gyrfalcon passed within binocular range. At first I discredited the identification. Impossible. No gyrfalcon ever abandoned an uncontested realm of polar tundra in mid-July—unless prolonged freakish weather had locked her out of her land. As a long-time bird-watcher, I scribbled a note of the sighting anyway.

While cutting and lugging armloads of herbs from the meadow, I made mental notes of transient impressions of canyon wildlife. Whenever careful observation revealed consistent trends, I recorded those items in my daybook. Scrupulous details afforded lengthy rest stops. The more fatigued I became, the more detailed became my recordings. And while on that subject, I must acknowledge frittering away an inordinate number of hours inhaling afternoon canyon whirlwinds deliciously laden with the essences of sage, balsam, lily, and clover. Frankly, the land made a bigger impression than the pikas; passing moose, elk, deer, bighorn sheep, and bear contended more effectively for the spotlight with their high visibility. Everything grew bigger than pikas. You had to look closely even to see one.

The most consistent trend was the ease with which I lapsed into themes of fancy, with too little regard for incidents that might sprout into important information. The intoxicating air, vibrating incessantly with song, movement, and bigness, frequently beckoned my attention away from the duty at hand.

On July 18, the fourth day of observation in Cragrockland, I became deeply absorbed in the infinite teamwork with which pairs of pikas chose and clipped units of fodder for winter garners. Perhaps I was cutting the wrong plants. Then suddenly the more exciting teamwork of paired goshawks attracted my attention—again because they were so much bigger. The tercel (male) created a shadow, soliciting a ruffed grouse's eye away from the sun; the falcon (female), with intense high-altitude glare behind her, taloned the grouse, then shared with her mate in co-operative feast on a nearby dead tamarack. Life in the Wind Rivers—a joint precision operation—demanded collective efficiency. The collectively vigilant survived.

Since I refused to accept the carnivorous lifestyle, I asked myself why it was that I had resisted a personal temptation to warn the grouse. Unconsciously Eagle Rock's admonition came to mind: "Neither influence nor encroach upon their lives." Never far from grazers, gleaners, and honey sippers, the ravenous eyes of carnivores reconnoitered each savory victim sometimes for days before an attack. Keen and patient fissipeds (a nontechnical and better term for mammal predators) focused acutely for that first sign of weakness. Perhaps a little of my interference might even sharpen the meat eaters' wit and improve them biologically. I wasn't about to allow any carnivore to sneak up on a pika—no matter what Eagle Rock said.

The final flicker of sundown's afterglow on that fourth day of observation compelled my reluctant return to camp. Lying on my belly by the firelight from dry squaw wood and resinous cones, I recorded notebook highlights of the day. At the same time, in spite of the bear's impatient paw gently tugging at my shoulder for a handout, I listed specific behavior patterns that so far characterized in my own mind *Ochotona princeps,* the pika.

Young and old alike, Square Top Mountain pikas embodied noisy little calliopes that bleated, whistled, or sang much of the time—night and day, according to what stood out in my mind as distinctly frivolous moods. Could the old shaman have thought of them as bohemians? Throughout Rockslideland their "eenk!" dominated other wildlife sounds. Their ways of vocal expression distinguished various individuals that had attained the knack of scaled differences in whistle, song, and subvocal hum. Their throaty chatter reached an amazing intensity, complete with what appeared to be associative meanings among different family groups. Simply by habit, I suppose, they soon lost most of their compunctions against vocalizing while I climbed about the talus.

Particular members of the colony appeared to volunteer their services as sentries—lookouts to whistle regular alert reminders even when no enemy stalked—a sign of intrinsic distrust that was no doubt associated with the pikas' industry on the open meadow where there was little cover and where agile raptors stooped and fissipeds closed without the slightest prior conveyance of intent. Wherever they worked, most pikas froze at selected signals, then betrayed their positions by haunching and whistling a medley of "tunes" as if denying the existence of real hunger in prowling enemies. Sentries relayed emergency messages across the "village" from one lookout post to the next, depending upon the direction of a carnivore's approach or their interpretation of a blue jay's sirened alarm.

At the end of the fifth day on the talus, I decided that pika behavior bypassed most human logic. At first they decided to ignore my presence. When they realized I would *not* be ignored, they adopted an attitude of, "Why don't you go away?" I think I detected some expressions of plain resignation. As I began sickling small bundles of herbs on the meadow near where they were harvesting, however, their reaction grew by degrees into a kind of tolerant curiosity. At times I fought off a distinct feeling they were laughing at me. Of course, this was a purely human response to an animal's deliberate snub. At least they no longer shrieked and hid when I offered granola, hamster treats, guinea pig pellets, or loads of harvested fodder, although they discarded most of what I cut for them. At sunset on July 19, several older members of the colony even approached my hand for the irresistible granola.

At campfire during the evening of that same fifth day, I examined a growing affection for the mild-mannered bear whom I taught to respond to the name Tatters. Dangling fur skeins, the result of summer molt, clung to his body like loose patches on a tattered old coat. In spite of Eagle Rock's order that I should chase him away, his easy friendship promoted my sense of belonging—even gave rise to a mild sense of responsibility for his welfare, at least while he slouched around camp of an evening. I threw stones at a pair of dive-bombing ravens that persisted in claiming Tatters's huge round fanny for a target. The well-behaved bear acted like a dog, and I looked forward to our nighttime campfire. He soon developed the habit of leaning against my side when I sat and allowed him to lick all the "kitchen" hardware. He now postponed his foraging for food until I retired to the sleeping bag. Before leaving camp, he sat near my head and grumbled for a few minutes as if annoyed at my inability to stay awake. One might suspect that his tendency to press physically close to a warm body he trusted reflected some instinct lingering from cubhood rather than budding love for a campfire man.

On the afternoon of July 20, I learned more about the nonpredaceous multitude and how each family from pika to moose cooperated with a system of comprehensive countryside alarms. Skimming a circuitous route barely above the meadow's vibrant summer green, the blue jay issued a raucous twang, a squawky summons to arms. The chanticleer bird glided swiftly to the lakes and back. The red-tailed hawk screamed in a fit of rage when every denizen of Cragrockland ducked for cover, having recognized salvation in the nosey jay's warning. I looked forward to an early eyeball "conference" with that dependable town crier. He removed my name from his dangerous-creatures-to-be-shunned list after a second peanut and raisin payoff.

Pikas respected the jay and reacted to his "bulletins" as they did to signals from their own sentries. Colonists on the talus rushed to their bunkers, while those on the meadow crouched rigidly under spiny umbrellas of gooseberry, eglantine, and buckthorn.

Out of nowhere on that afternoon of the twentieth, a rocketlike raptor executed a parabolic flight pattern, then stooped earthward for 1,000 feet at about 150 miles an hour. At the close the falcon all but deplumed a band-tailed pigeon. For days I speculated upon the possible reasons the pigeon had disregarded a combination of the blue jay's alarm and a whisky-jack's warning trumpet.

My first sighting had been accurate after all. It was indeed a gyrfalcon! Earth's fastest and most intelligent bird. Largest of the arctic hawks, last species to go south in autumn. Only some mysterious adversity of the direst sort on her northern muskeg could have driven that polar monarch from her native heath to an impoverished Wyoming bivouac in July. In a month's time the formidable killer and her tercel could exterminate the pika colony and other small mammal communities in the region of Green River lakes.

On the afternoon of the falcon, the heat developed a creepy, gummy quality that permeated stone, shadow, forest, and flesh. Wispy cloud banners fingered at the toothy peaks and contrailed warpaths for the mercurial west wind. Toward sundown, yeasty cumuli kneaded their masses against the mountains, discharging sufficient electrical current to whittle boulders from 2,000-foot cliffs. Dry lightning shattered granite outcroppings, splintered 200-year-old tamaracks—but not a drop of rain fell. An unusual smell of dryness permeated the atmosphere.

Perimetered by basinland desert on all sides, this homeland of the pika resembles no other mountainous region in the Western Hemisphere. The range itself stands aloof, abominating every inroad of change incompatible with nature's long evolution by trial and error.

Initiated from birth into the rigorous, unbridled fury of Wind River Mountain climate, the unimpressible pikas looked on with quiet dignity from boulder tops while throughout the canyon other species scattered in panic at the onset of a reckless summer thunderstorm before dark that day. Discharges of thunder and lightning stampeded Tatters into deep hiding somewhere near the upper Green River Lake, and nothing short of an ill-tempered grizzly could have rousted him from his secret refuge until the storm had passed. Even though he smelled my milk chocolate pot and knew it contained generous "leavings," he bawled and raced away as if pursued by demons. In a warm dry cave he probably fell asleep and forgot about the whole thing. The next morning he returned to the campsite, however, with an empty belly, a ravenous appetite, and an unclouded memory of the milk chocolate he had left behind. He "danced" on his hind paws with excitement when he learned I had saved the treat for him.

The Synergic Society

The day after the dry thunderstorm, the pikas often interrupted their harvesting on the meadow in order to flash unanimous glances my way—almost as if they wished to impart a message. Wishful thinking on my part. Their unusual torrent of bandied chitchat seemed to indicate they might consider an end to snubbing me. To restate an earlier observation, the more I studied them the deeper the interest they generated. In point of fact, within that week of observation they had earned my profound respect for their industry, consistency, and genteel behavior. The gyrfalcon's appearance may have coincided with an internal clock that triggered the colony to more systematic cutting from the meadow's abundance—to conveying six to twelve-inch stems to their bunkers. From sunrise until sunset they now cut, dried, and wove mature provender into bushel-basket-sized stacks—the winter ricks or granaries Eagle Rock called garners.

And although they appeared deliberately to ignore my warning overtures in pointing out soaring raptors, they browsed and worked with less wildness and skittishness the more I walked or crawled among them. Velvet-eyed glances even revealed elementary interest in my presence at long last. Perhaps a beginning of communication. Although unable to analyze their mood, I sensed an intangible change in their attitude on the twenty-first. They allowed me to sit and rest with them without signs of nervousness. They chattered incessantly and all at the same time. If pikas have a language—I said to myself in exasperation—they never give anyone a chance to understand one "word."

Toward late afternoon eight older pikas followed me to the meadow and goggled like English judges each time I mowed and tied to my aluminum packframe thick shocks containing stems and leaves of every available plant. When the load eventually arrived at the foot of a flat slab the size and shape of a large dining room table near the top of the talus—my own friendly "Meditation Tower" or "Ponder Rock"—the same older pikas followed and tore the sheaf apart, discarding more than half its bulk while staring me squarely in the eyes. They carried the remainder by mouth for sun curing on rocks above their family dens. I had carefully listed every species of plantlife they were cropping, eighteen different varieties—everything from short sedges, grasses, and ferns to long goldenrod panicles and fireweed racemes. I thought I understood what they wanted. I didn't. Perhaps they might communicate—if my patience survived those daffy days of probation.

To continue reaping and delivering with only half-acceptable results, however, would require expenditure of physical and mental effort beyond human endurance.

Therefore, on the way to camp that evening, I vowed to observe more carefully and to avoid premature conclusions concerning the plants they wanted to cure. There had to be a cue because we were harvesting the same species; yet they discarded much of what I carried.

How those little goblins could work! With only an occasional breather, they spiraled down to the meadow and back up the talus. They knew the critical state of ripeness in each plant and its capacity to cure correctly for maximum sustenance yield throughout the winter. Instinctively they understood that a family of four required 160 pounds of dry food before new growth could sprout on the meadow after the June thraw. In addition to the task of building *family* stacks, adult workers interlaced the sun-toasted hay, one well-placed branch at a time, into *community* garners along what I called "Main Street" of the "village," about sixty feet down the talus from the Ponder Rock. The pikas handled with care what they acquired through hard labor.

According to my notes, haying time coincided with ripening season for sedges, grasses, and specific forbs. The third week in July, for instance, represented critical maturity for yarrow, wheat grass, miner's lettuce, wild onion, sorrel cress, cassiope, shooting star, and fireweed. Although the subtundra included a rich number of plant species, their growing periods at that altitude rarely exceeded four weeks.

Only two and one-half seasons constituted a year in the alpine zone of the Wind River Range: six weeks of spring, an abbreviated five or six weeks of autumn, and about forty weeks of winter. Summer was nonexistent. The last week of "spring" and the first week of "autumn" brought steamy hot days and chilly nights.

After several recalculations, I sat upright and stared into space, shocked at the monumental task the pikas faced. Wasted time suddenly symbolized heresy none of us could afford during the short haying season that remained.

From the pika position at Square Top Mountain, loss of time could result in delayed curing because of fewer sunny hours in August than in July—and therefore a better than even chance to starve. According to the Shoshone shaman, environmental misfortunes—weather, predation, parasites, competitors, cataclysms—have elevated the pikas, fortified them with such attributes as toughness, tenderness, integrity, even as suffering has elevated men and women.

All too frequently the Earth Mother plunges with headlong speed to protect her creatures from weather, hastens with every means of assault to defend them against enemies, works incessantly to shore up their homes against accidental calamity, then lavishes upon them the time required to die of starvation. Occasionally I found myself severely at odds with Eagle Rock's Earth Mother.

On the morning of July 23, I studied a third-quarter new moon as it dropped toward the western crestline a little more than an hour before sunrise was due over the eastern wall. I fell back into deep sleep while both cold lights glowed on two horizons at the same time. Shortly before sunup I awoke in mute astonishment to find eighteen stark-eyed pikas balancing on their haunches, completely surrounding my sleeping bag at somewhat less than four feet away.

They had uttered no sound to awaken me. Except for the gurgling Lagomorph Creek and a clique of leathery-tongued aspens giggling in the predawn breeze, the tableau was as silently rigid as sculpture. My impression must have reflected an empty dishpan stare, perhaps a gawk of mingled surprise and disbelief. Every pika's face indicated, to me at least, entreaty. Entreaty it was, not a bargain. Man is the only animal that bargains. At any rate, I leaned first on one elbow, then on the other, agonizing to appraise the spectacle. What on earth would bring eighteen wild animals to my sleeping bag at sunrise? Eighteen trouble-eyed leprechauns were trying to communicate an appeal for help. Obviously. I assumed that carnivores had raised galvanic hell during darktime in Rockslideland. Except for the creek's lonely monotone, stony silence had reigned throughout the night.

After stuffing aching muscles into the tangle of my clothing, then grabbing a breakfast handful of granola and dried apricots, I stumbled after the apprehensive swarm that urged me to follow toward the talus. On the meadow a solitary swallowtail butterfly was riding piggyback on the first golden shaft of sunlight.

When the pikas began shattering every crevice of canyon silence with choral exercises, that tatterdemalion yearling bear leaped into my mind. I hoped he would stay away until the colonists could reach the rocky side of the heath. Bears eat pikas. I hated the prospect of having to work on Tatters's rear end with an alpenstock.

Perhaps it was a naive notion—a sudden burst of wishful thinking—but suddenly I felt sure those little knights and ladies of the talus ramparts embodied feelings, thoughts, and integrity. Like Tatters, they personified a kindred force, now that they had ventured to my sleeping bag—with a message. I groped for definitions. One solitary assumption became a fact: They had stolen into camp in order to accompany me to the harvest. They sought no refuge from any ravaging carnivore!

As a matter of record, the pikas had definitely accomplished one timid step toward intelligent communication.

Even if completely out of character with pika zeal for isolation, their appearance in camp exemplified what ethologists call *reversal behavior*, not uncommon among denizens of deep wilderness in time of recognized need. There remained little doubt that the colony had faced a proposition and had reached a decision. I became further convinced when individuals scrambled back and forth to "teach" me several routines essential to the service they solicited.

Skeptics may insist that the phenomena that followed were coincidences; nevertheless, I shall record precisely what took place with neither embellishment nor omission. In a manner that I fell short of comprehending at the time, the pikas sensed my profound wonder when I recognized that they had accepted an offer of help—a bona fide communication I had imparted to them, unaware of broadcasting a message. The thought had flowed without restraint or confusion from my eyes and my activities. It had registered on their brains. On more occasions than I can remember, they had studied my eyes. Their appearance in camp and subsequent activity on the meadow manifested an instinctive response to my efforts, a reply that I had convinced them I had been offering help with their problem.

Back and forth they scooted, a charming throng, scampering through matted vegetation almost in regimented unison. As morning advanced, each member of the lilliputian community enthusiastically delegated himself to pass in front of me with a clipped stem in his or her mouth, thus showing me which plants to sickle and the desired ripeness of the wanted stem. We had achieved initial understanding. We now pitched into the harvest together as a team. Sprinting in front of my boots with a mouthful of three-awn, wheat grass, sedge, goldenrod, or owl's clover, they looked up as if delighted with the arrangement.

The task entailed labor far more coarse and exacting than I had anticipated. There was no alternative. They watched every move I made. They forced me to copy them, to cut *only* the fragrant, ripe-stemmed crop of their choice. With shrill barks they prevented me from chopping primrose, saxifrage, and chicory not yet ripe; but regardless of how diligently I studied their requirements, when we arrived at garners high on the talus, they continued to eliminate much from my heavy shocks before spreading the remainder to cure. Even Eagle Rock, after his lengthy study of pikas, had admitted never having quite mastered their rigid mandates and requirements. As a younger man, he was never able to keep up with them physically. In addition to boundless energy, the Earth Mother had endowed her midgets with rich knowledge about the rules of harvesting, curing, and warehousing food. A rudiment of reason seemed to creep in and govern their appetites—except when they gobbled thistles, eglantine, and buckthorn—no doubt a reasonable indulgence from their standpoint.

The pikas appeared to have granted me that one day of intensively tutored apprenticeship; thereafter, they may have expected me to perform as a member journeyman. July 23 was a day to remember for a lifetime. The atmosphere remained hypnotic. A spicy aura of sun-toasted fodder clung to the steep hillside, because for once the wind was deviling around somewhere else. A rhythmic, saucy lilt ran through the pikas' worktime humming as the friendly little creatures toiled. Even the timeless rigidity and roughness of their rocky homeland now seemed less awesome. Light, warmth, and song—an unmistakable pulse of life itself—penetrated every cranny. Out of breath most of the time, perspiration clouding my vision, I managed to harmonize a little whistling with their humming on *downhill* runs; but under heavy loads during *uphill* climbs, we carried on with the seriousness of drill sergeants. For once every detail of the day rang of perfection.

That night I shared a dehydrated stew with the well-mannered Tatters. After we had eaten, I fell asleep on top of the sleeping bag, too tired to undress. When I awakened about midnight, the bear was still sitting near my head. He left when I crawled inside the sleeping bag.

At dawn eighteen wily pikas again crept slowly and silently into camp and surrounded the sleeping bag. I expected them and was therefore peeping through the slit between my right eyelids when the swarm crept up to where I lay. They remained as still as tombstones until I revealed that I was awake. They stared in keen-eyed silence while I prepared and ate hot cornmeal mush and cocoa. Unafraid of the campfire, probably because Eagle Rock had introduced them to it, they followed me everywhere, even to the creek where they chattered the clear syllables of disbelief among themselves while I took an icy sponge bath. Once back on the meadow, however, they raised their voices in what I interpreted to be a community sing-along. I said a little prayer of thanks to my own Gitche Manito for baby-sitting with Tatters in another canyon.

After each sweaty delivery of freshly cut provender, I sprawled out for a few minutes on the warm Meditation Tower near the cliff and waited for a return of breath and energy. With much exertion, human lungs gulp for oxygen at 10,000 feet above sea level. Exhibiting the speed and dexterity of Flemish lace makers, the pikas shuttled back and forth, tending their fodder, periodically turning, straightening, untangling, spreading. Then they scurried to nearby boulders and sat, motionless but zealously alert while they rested and waited for me to resume my assignment. They went out of their way to look me squarely in the eyes as I climbed from the massive platform to rejoin them in the urgent chore.

They must have learned from experience that if they closed their eyes during a rest period, the golden eagle would stoop; he studied their expressions from his perch half a mile across the canyon. The pikas had adequate eyesight with which to watch the big raptor from that distance. Eventually they appeared to appreciate the rest stop I demanded between loads.

Although nothing beyond a shaky strategy for survival bound us together yet, the colonists gurgled and leaped with enthusiasm every time we approached my Meditation Tower. The huge flat boulder soon symbolized for me—and I believe for the pikas as well—a plateau of friendship. From my Cherokee father I learned to love certain rocks as if they were living entities. Throughout the West, I have made friends with a host of big, comfortable, confidential boulders.

Even as avalanche lilies distributed their fragrance on the mountain air, so did those little puffs of song and softness diffuse their influence on me—a steady permeation, ever so slight at first but soon tremendous and overpowering. When in a receptive state of mind, I felt completely humble before them. My Amerind relatives have often spoken of the humility they always sustain when they address an animal.

On the first afternoon when a half dozen pikas joined me on Meditation Tower, I lost all feeling of fatigue. Their trust and friendship soothed every cramp, blister, and aching muscle. Their confidence and open-faced honesty transcended the cleft between our species and elevated human attitudes toward a new pinnacle of humility. A superb sense of wonder always soars within the human heart when an animal of any kind manifests friendly trust.

My incessant fear of inadvertently stepping, stumbling, or falling on a pika as we descended the steep, unstable talus developed into a dreadful phobia, often to return at night under the hood of hounding nightmares. Half the rocks and boulders on the slope gave the impression of being loose, poised to tip, roll, and crash to the meadow with the slightest nudge—to destroy every living animal in their paths. No one could possibly understand that horrible feeling without having seen the little beasts milling almost shoulder to shoulder at my feet and staring up into my eyes as we moved back to work. They scrambled for attention, possibly to let me know how satisfied they were with our work together. Innately too gentle ever to jostle or shove one another, most of the throng spent whatever time they could afford, so it appeared, struggling to make themselves individually known to me. And they did just that.

Despite periods of wild elation, what the end of those first long days did to my physical body bordered upon the grotesque. Toward evening, each round trip took more time and determination than the preceding. Demanding to move up and down the talus as a unit (probably a means to foil predation), the pikas often refused to leave the meadow with their half dozen stems each until I tied and shouldered my bundle. When I shrieked for time out to recover my breath, to rub a cramping tendon, or to pierce a blister, they stood motionless on their haunches and whispered among themselves as solemn as Puritan deacons. They gurgled an unmistakable complaint—a kind of high-keyed bark—if I loitered. They pushed me subtly even when my body demanded recess. Time at that late date had grown too precious for them to throw it away on human inactivity.

Bitch-wolf hungry, tired to the marrow, throat cracked from dehydration, I often glanced up at the glittering glaciers on Mount Sacajawea and promised to carry on—even when the sandblasted boulders on the talus focused into my eyes a sun-faceted mosaic of torture. By the pikas' instinct, every day's work began at sunrise and terminated at sunset. They became unusually friendly at the close of day. Then, as the shaman had said, they had sense enough to climb the great Ponder Rock with me and face the sunset spectacle, refusing to move until the afterglow had faded. The extra effort they seemed to demand right up until the sun went down, as well as the close association that followed, kept a question bounding around in my mind: Were they trying to communicate again, especially at sunset?

At that time, I still speculated upon a more fancy-free attitude toward enjoying the colonists rather than trying to understand them. But they appeared to savor a message they wished to share. They knew something I didn't. An inordinate amount of hard work on my part went into understanding that "bulletin." Indeed, every intuitive glance indicated an important "statement" in those expressive eyes, a declaration, so to speak, yet I was not quite ready to receive it. A narrow but deep chasm still separated us; and frankly, I hesitated to jump across to their side for fear of discovering something that might undermine my human prejudices. For the moment I gave up trying to decode the sunset messages for fear of indulging in a sentimental anthropomorphic attitude!

At first it was difficult for me to avoid gestures habitually employed with both head and hands at the same time. Movement of the extremities startled the pikas, whereas vocal and optical signals imparted confidence. During periods of frustration, my conventional background acquired since college days stood out as an age-old barrier between us. My book learning prevented immediate and honest, if not semantic, lingua franca for correspondence. The pikas demonstrated more patient understanding and less hurry.

While toting heavy shocks of green hay over steep talus boulders or drudging down to the meadows for another load, I may have underestimated the importance of several observations. On one occasion the colony ceased to chatter in order to regard me in unanimous silence. They stopped abruptly an important activity of the moment and stared up into my unresponsive gaze. Their eyes were like polished zircon buttons. Eagle Rock would have known what to do. Tall Feather would have known. I didn't get it. I was too far removed to realize that something substantial tugged at their minds.

Further doubt persisted. Was it truly possible that Amerinds communicated intelligently with nonlinguistic animals, performing the prodigious transaction optically with only occasional help from body signals and gestures? And, assuming that Eagle Rock had communicated with wildlife—after all, I *saw* the birds at Sacajawea's grave—could other human beings learn to do the same?

In the back of my head I still pooh-poohed answers to those questions. Nevertheless, in view of what sparkled in pikas' eyes, I was puzzled enough to cling seriously to the beguiling curiosity. We may have accepted unrealistically that no animal could possibly converse to any appreciable length with one of a different species. We may have rejected unreasonably the masses of literature on extrasensory perception among different species. The pikas appeared to be at the point of communicating.

Intuition and memory no doubt govern the pika mind more than any other factors beyond instinct. The so-called sixth sense approximates another term for intuition. Most birds and mammals "think" on a sixth-sense basis. Although curiosity often regulates the extent to which first-step behavior goes, memory of specific consequences from previous involvements heavily influences further initiatory learning. Curiosity, first and most rudimentary of all complex emotional motivators, functions in reality not only as a measure of an individual's appetite and capacity for learning but also as a forerunner of reason. Curiosity carried to its logical conclusion results in a desire to communicate. All discovery—including the discovery of communication itself—has flowed from the fountainhead of innate (evolved) curiosity, differing in quantity and quality within each entity.

Whether he intended to or not, Eagle Rock provided certain clues for the study of voiceless intercommunication when he elaborated upon his early parental training. Both his parents had schooled him in receptiveness, in nonverbal transmission of thought fragments through facial expression of what lay behind the eyes. It must be borne in mind that his parents had received training from an all-time master of optical communication, none other than Bird Woman, Sacajawea Charbonneau, who, according to Eagle Rock, "spoke" with birds.

Eagle Rock had emphasized the infinite variety in dumb language—body signals transmitted to another's eyes in absolute silence. The more sophisticated the system, the more extensive its survival value for those who apply it in daily confrontations.

Thus, in command of a complicated signal system, the pika had a better chance for longevity than the pigeon, who depended more upon camouflage when the gyrfalcon hunted than upon communicated warnings. In the dominion of silent correspondence, a little more knowledge would certainly destroy none of the magic of wonder.

In order to interpret those fascinating catchlights reflected from pika eyes—and body semaphores flashed my way—I decided then and there to attend pika "kindergarten," if they saw fit to indulge me, to begin with the simplest impulses, to memorize every combination of cues they employed, to advance exclusively in *their* idiom until winter drove me out.

Ridding myself of intellectual resistance and conventional ties to human traditions proved a far more shattering experience than one might imagine. Perhaps it encompassed new adventure for the pikas themselves, beyond what Eagle Rock had already done to narrow the no-man's land between pika and human. I hoped the colonists would recognize similarities as well as differences between the two human personalities.

Although many natural barriers blocked my course, progress was swift and intense. One day I became so engrossed in the experiment and the pikas' obvious disposition to teach that darkness was setting in before I realized noon had passed. For some reason, the colonists had neglected to lead me to the Ponder Rock for the sunset. When I reached camp, Tatters stood upright near my sleeping bag. Hoping to find out what he wanted, I walked directly to him. He tapped my shoulders with his forepaws and stared into my eyes with the most startling expression I had ever seen on an animal's face. He wished to communicate—for him, no innovation. Before that week, I had clung categorically to skepticism regarding optical conveyance of thought. Facing the bear less than twelve inches from his muzzle, I felt immeasurably helpless, unable yet to read any kind of message directed specifically to my eyes. A tediously long distance stood between me and the time when I might hope for one rational meaning in an animal's silent expression.

Dialect of the Eyes

Agitated and impatient because I could not comprehend the message he beamed, the indignant Tatters slouched into the bulky shadows, where he sputtered and gabbled to himself. At that moment I must have been much less than inspiring company. After supper he jabbered near the fire pit and eyed me unflinchingly while he licked generous leavings from an aluminum pot. I lowered the rucksack from a bearproof branch and handed him a double graham cracker smeared with honey as a lopsided reward for staying off the talus and meadow during those first crucial days when my rapport with the pikas dangled in exasperatingly fragile balance. It suddenly flashed across my mind that I had ordered Tatters off the meadow that very day for fear he might seize a trusting pika. His communication may have solicited a logical reason for my having gone against nature by evicting him from his own heath. My logic bothered him only in that he could not comprehend it; to my knowledge, he never again wandered near the talus after that expulsion.

No claims intended. It simply worked out that way.

Neither sentiment nor prejudiced viewpoint prompts me to state that during my stay at Square Top Mountain Tatters and I founded a friendship closer than that between a man and his dog. Rare indeed were the times when we failed to make one another understand. Regardless of pain and fatigue from the harvest, I always bestowed an appropriate expression of applause when he met me at camp. A good round of ear boxing, wrestling, dunking in the creek, sparring—anything as long as it was basically rough—expressed applause to Tatters. And I always rewarded him when he made me understand an important message. Rewards were invariably symbolized in sweet chocolate. Tatters thrived on approbation. Not having known him, you can only partially imagine his volcanic delight and satisfaction when approbation was combined with chocolate.

Haunched near the campfire, he swayed and moaned to the tunes of old Spanish waltzes I played for him on the harmonica. When not half-dead from the day's labor, I walked with him on his forage range as far as upper Green River Lake. Our way of bidding good-night was an exchange of friendly swats to the head! The idea was to see who could get in the last swat before the other got away. Throughout the course of our time together, he was rarely less than the finest company a man could want. Our friendship and understanding never reached a plateau where it leveled off; it continued to grow. In disgust Eagle Rock stated much later that Tatters and I deserved each other.

Like a Saint Bernard puppy, the bear craved affection. Each time we wrestled, he tussled and sparred rougher than any human opponent—I never made his league—but his roughness merely manifested boundless inwrought enthusiasm and the ursine hankering to press physically close. After one haymaker to the nose, he got the message that nobody would tolerate a bear's "gentle" habit of sneaking up to the sleeping bag at 3:00 A.M. and startling the daylights out of the snoring chocolate provider with a generous lick across the face.

Although the abandoned orphan possessed ample capacity for learning and remembering, the greater part of his wilderness schooling entailed either pain or shock. One morning before daylight I awoke to find the moaning bear haunched at my head. A flashlight beam revealed six shiny porcupine quills embedded in the fleshy tissue of his nose. He stood on his hind legs for our little greeting ceremony when I crawled from the sleeping bag—a gentle face-slapping contest that lasted perhaps thirty seconds. He then allowed me to grasp the first two-inch quill. All I could do was tear it out as quickly as possible. Before I could duck, his uncontrollable swat sent me sprawling to the ground. He bawled for forgiveness each of the seven times he knocked me down—once for each quill and once for the iodine swab. For my efforts I nursed twenty-seven claw welts on my back, chest, and arms, and four painful "goose eggs" on my head.

Meanness and ingratitude were nonexistent in Tatters, but his one-track reaction to sudden pain was to hit back with his paw. Later that day I discovered the dead porcupine, one to whom I had given pinches of salt when he visited camp. Upon examining the limping bear's paw, I found where he had extracted five quills with his teeth. Another swat for another swab of iodine!

On one of our moonlight hikes to the upper lake, we met a cranky-faced, fifty-pound beaver who refused us right-of-way on the trail. I have forgotten why we believed we were entitled to it; the beaver was traveling uphill. More curious than annoyed, the bear approached the big rodent for a get-acquainted sniff. With speed and dexterity not usually associated with his species, the beaver executed an about-face and clobbered Tatters across the nose bridge with his heavy paddlelike tail. Had I not restrained the bear, he would have killed the beaver before the impudent beast could have reached safety in the lake. Until the end of our hike, however, Tatters nipped my arms and legs, swatted me repeatedly, and kept up a running vocal denunciation until we returned to camp, to all of which I pretended not the slightest recognition. I had established my position when the bear accepted restraint at the scene of his embarrassment; and while he vented steam against my person for more than a mile, he never again nettled that resident beaver. In my notes I called the profitable episode a lesson in "successful communication."

An amusing surprise occurred shortly before dark on Saturday, July 25, that same week. At Tatters's insistence, I followed him up the game trail along the right bank of Lagomorph Creek. From his expression and cunning demeanor, his running to me, looking ahead, running again, it was plain enough that he wished to involve me in mischief he felt unable to handle by himself. At the small meadow a quarter mile above camp, Tatters reared, looked back at me, then proceeded cautiously on four paws—the signal for me to follow silently. Halfway across the meadow a pair of high-plumed skunks were feasting on grasshoppers, caterpillars, and mice. The yearling had no doubt scouted the skunks' activities for some time. To my surprise he wobbled up to the well-armed couple and nudged the larger one none too gently. Either the native instinct of all intelligent woodland creatures deserted him at that moment or he believed my concurrence in his scheme would somehow prevent the inevitable. Reeling under the accurate marksmanship of both skunks, the bear sent the couple rolling across the meadow, then disappeared toward the creek. I saw no more of him until the following Monday evening, at which time he belly-crawled up to my campfire, still reeking of musk, still probably galled that I had allowed the indignity to befall him. His utterances included sounds I hadn't heard before from *any* bear.

Occasionally after full days as harvester and dray-man, my withered condition prevented playing the "Green River Steinway" for the bear or accompanying him on a hike. Tatters understood. He let me know that he under-stood by leaning against me and gurgling soft little "tunes" of his own. On those evenings, after the quickest possible meal of raisin corn dodger, Spam, and a cup of cocoa, I surrendered generous remains and the utensils to the bear. While he licked the supper gear, I wormed into the mummy bag. He deplored a *short* evening by the fire or a *short* hike. Gladly would he have given up his nighttime forage had I sat or hiked with him.

Fatigue and sleeplessness sometimes reinforced one another to surfeit the province of worry. Worry always advanced the purchase price of trouble before payment became due. But I continued to fret over the pikas' insolu-ble problem: *time.* In the days remaining before frost, sim-ple mathematics showed that approximately twenty-five colonists had to cure 1,200 pounds—dry weight—of proper silage: 160 man-loads at thirty pounds a load be-fore drying. To find. To reap. To bind. To deliver by climbing a treacherous slope composed of sharp, blinding, blocking, unstably anchored boulders for a distance of 250 to 420 yards. Five loads a day for thirty-two days—on condition ideal weather persisted without interruption, provided the drought eased off, provided the fodder held out, provided competitors stayed off the meadow. With cheerful zeal the pikas carried their share, but time had eroded their chances of success. And therein festered the worry that jeopardized badly needed sleep.

Tall Feather often repeated an old Cherokee saw that

used to infuriate me as a youngster: "The man who rises of a morning without starlight in his eyes will lose his race with time." Now it made sense.

Weather-front cumuli from the Pacific Northwest blew in and spewed wispy white banners off the gusty brows of the divide. Because of the drought, I wanted to cheer should rain fall; but because of the harvest, I feared costly delay. To make up for time lost during bad weather, each rainy day would levy an extra load of winter staples every day for five days.

I also worried because of the increasing army of carnivores who were hanging around the canyon. The pikas probably knew about the newcomer foxes that prowled over the talus with impunity. The stealthy pair slunk in and out of view, emboldened by summer prestorm conditions and the two-legger who hurled *stones*, not bullets. Inasmuch as the hunger monster motivated all carnivores in the same way, the fearless foxes, like owls, might try to intercept my little friends on their way to awaken me before the starlight left the sky. Foxes never took long to acquire new techniques.

Another worry brought about some extra hours of lost sleep: If cold-air cloud banners were now trailing southeast of the Continental Divide with consistency, it would require less than a week for frost to expel ungulate bucks—deer, wapiti, and bighorn sheep—from their crestline downs. They would join their does and ewes on lower altitude braes and meadows alo)ng the river, especially if the drought continued. Not only would invasive grazers deplete our meadow by eating a large portion of it, but also their excretions would force the pikas to reject most remaining herbage. I suspected the qualmish Little Chiefs had already discarded much of my earlier deliveries because they detected latent urinous and fecal odors I had no way of recognizing.

After a night of distorting worry, it struck me that I

had barely dozed off when eight pairs of superbly simple, fathomless eyes shocked me back to consciousness.

"Slave drivers!" I whispered so as not to startle the pudgy little gnomes. "It's not even graylight. Look at the stars!" Tall Feather's admonition.

When I rolled over to ignore them for another ten-minute snooze, there stood eight more pikas haunched on that side of the sleeping bag. Pikas rarely haunched either on the talus or on the meadow. They crouched unless they supposed that very grave circumstances of the moment warranted a haunch.

After several yawns, I got up and maneuvered into clothing that Tatters had scattered from hell to breakfast during the night. I don't know what he was looking for, but he was certainly due for another meaningful communication. I scowled. The pika troop whispered. A few minutes passed before I realized that no equivalent for *scowl* existed in their "semantics."

They may have read my whole face, as Eagle Rock claimed to have done. I had begun to feel transparent in front of the little pixies. Their expressions remained unchanging while I tied my clammy boots in the half-light. I shouldered the packframe and rope for carrying sheaves, grabbed a box of dry cereal, and prepared to follow my

relentless mentors to the meadow. No further question existed that empathy, if not communication, flowed among us like electric current through copper netting. As a matter of record, I *enjoyed* transparency in front of the animal eye.

As we worked the meadow, I soon forgot the vexation of early rising and the specters of drought, rain, predation, and competition. Exhilaration swept over me as I looked into thirty-two sparkling eyes upturned my way. Sixty-four little feet scurried to keep pace. The agreeable fancy also occurred to me that had it not been for predawn reveille, I might have missed the wildest rapture in summertime bird music: songfests that poured from trees and meadow between 4:30 and 5:30 A.M.

Almost like the physical relief a snake must feel when it sheds an old skin, I sustained new freedom, shedding one by one the scales of prejudice, pretense, and convention in order to link mentally with the colony and Tatters. Every day I awoke more aware that nature and man coincided more closely than most people realized—that complicated human abstracts too often walled out many of the natural joys inbred in simplicity.

In order to know the pikas one from another, I had to find characteristics of personality and minute physical details peculiar to each one. About twenty out of thirty—the exact number of Square Top Mountain pikas appeared to be a colonial secret—looked like carbon-copy-type animals until I seriously came to grips with each personality. Sooner than expected—and with what I interpreted as their help—I fixed differences in sizes and markings, in greetings, in the ways they moved or bore their burdens, in capacities and willingness to empathize, in many little ways that distinguished entities. For reference convenience, I gave them names in the record book.

Toughy and Skippy stood out as the largest mated pair in the colony—hard workers, taciturn, always out front, always alert. I needed a reliable right-hand helper couple on the talus. That couple turned out to be Toughy and Skippy. Calculating their ages on the basis of body development, fur, physical condition, and general appearance, I estimated them to be about four years old. Skippy's enthusiasm for work and friendly association with her kind persuaded me to believe that she enjoyed life with boundless verve. Toughy may have been Skippy's mental inferior in some ways, but no pika could outdo him when it came to delivering fodder to the talus. He almost never reacted as rapidly as Skippy. The couple rarely left my sight from dawn to sunset.

Shiny wore the glossiest coat in the colony. He was a chronic complainer. He fussed no matter how little time I took between sleeping bag and packrack. He sometimes carried double loads, as though he felt the colony would benefit by his extra labor. He may have been setting an example for those who, according to his standards, were not doing their share because he grumbled bitterly when he saw any pika carry less. I had to go along with his faultfinding when I discovered that he and his mate were in the process of constructing garners where other colonists could feed from them come winter.

Bouncy was Shiny's mate. Like Skippy, she bounded over acres of ground; but, unlike Skippy, she accomplished very little beyond respectable motherhood. It was most interesting to watch her teach her youngsters to harvest. She never allowed one of them to carry as little as she carried. In the neutral Earth Mother's eyes, Bouncy must have epitomized the ideal pika. She reproduced and trained efficient pikas.

Smiley glowed with good nature. He stood to one side and allowed others to pass. The first pika ever to sit on my lap during a rest stop at Meditation Tower, he showed me how a pika "smiled." The pika "smile," of course, is not a smile in the human sense. Smiley simply exhibited a pleasant look of satisfaction with life as we locked gazes.

Bitsy was the smallest and cuddliest adult in the colony. As Smiley's mate, she was old enough to have birthed at least five generations of healthy replacements for predation. The pair were both white around the mouth, a sure sign of age. Bitsy's forte shone in the example she set for industry, sharing, and obvious affection for other pikas. Through vigor, consistency, and diligence she must have inspired pikakind with an amazing amount of comfort. It was no accident that so many of the colony crowded around her for no reason other than company.

Mousey sang with the one foreign accent in the "village." His whistle registered as a high-fidelity squeak. Therefore, by mutual agreement, he projected his most valuable service to the community in a position of outer-wall sentry. Even I could distinguish between Mousey's "eenk" and another's.

Scotty was Mousey's mate. A model of frugality, she collected every stem that other pikas dropped. While Mousey did sentry duty, Scotty worked busily along with the rest of us, as though she were trying to harvest and carry her share and Mousey's at the same time. At least that's the way I imagined it. Between trips to the meadow, invariably she scudded to her mate's lookout post as if to reassure herself that he was bearing up under his "heavy" duty. At regular intervals the pair called back and forth while she worked on the meadow or trimmed the family's drying fodder.

Probably possessing sufficient personal virtue to stand alone, Temerarius occupied a unique position as bachelor hermit. And although he wanted even less to do with me than with pika folk, he never refused to lay out for curing the provender I deposited alongside his bunker—never turned down a fistful of guinea pig pellets or hamster treats. He toiled with the rest of us, but maintained a strictly hermitic life style. Pikas—and the two-legger with pellets—rendered him greatest service and made him happiest by ignoring his existence.

Although slight color variations were evident here and there, Spot stood out with a white blotch on her chest. Crusty, her mate, a big pika with nerve and verve like Toughy, had long guard hairs that grew above his downy pelt like a crust. In their clear eyes and shared activities, the pair reflected an expression that life was both a privilege and a pleasure. The fact that they wore such expressions on their countenances gave me the idea that such was their "philosophy." Every day I watched those two visit other pika families on the talus, possibly to encourage the less endowed or help where reinforcement was needed. I saw them visit family bunkers after a weasel or an owl had taken a brood member. One morning I was unable to locate Spot among the harvesters. At length I discovered the little doe performing extra duty as baby-sitter while parents of a young brood harvested and spread green stems for curing. Baby-sitting in the talus community occurred regularly and was frequently performed by older pikas unable to keep up the harvest rigors for more than half a day at a time.

It seemed strange until I gave it more ponder time on the rock, but Drummer remained an old maid—probably because she thumped hard with her hind legs against whatever surface she happened to squat upon. Under other circumstances—and between fidgety thumps—she whistled, sang, and chattered. Granting that she knew how to be silent when silence, safety, and virtue were synonymous, eligible bachelors avoided her as if she wore porcupine quills. Therefore, her compulsive thumping may have resulted only from the seismic aftershocks of spinsterhood. Drummer performed one questionable "village" service: She hurled shrieks that I interpreted as invective at two local sluggards each time she passed their ingeniously chosen crib at the corner I called First and Main on the upper talus, where pika families stored the most bountiful ricks of provender.

In my journal I listed the two sluggards as Mopish and Cadger, two country squires of advanced age, quite above or beyond work of any strain. They ate regularly, though—consuming other pikas' food. On rare occasions when Mopish didn't apear to be moping, he condescended to walk slowly to the meadow and back—perhaps for the exercise or for ripe strawberries. I never saw him eat a thistle or a gooseberry stem—or deliver any replacement supplies to Main Street garners where he leeched his meals. Cadger rarely moved beyond the bouldered collar of his den. Until I knew him better, I assumed he was an all-out sponger. During past winters, the two loafers apparently had sustained no serious trouble. Icy stares and Drummer's "insults" probably greeted the two poseurs whenever they showed up to dine on someone else's labor. Still they ate.

Toughy's and Skippy's daily attention to Cadger's food needs was one of the most touching I had ever observed, although I have read of many examples of similar behavior among a wide variety of animals. Careful scrutiny soon revealed to me that Cadger was all but totally *blind.*

My log book often refers to two friendly little yearling does, Peppy and Rally. The two served the talus as a genuine *pep rally* when spirits sometimes dipped to low ebb. Both Peppy and Rally seemed furtively to glad-eye Temerarius. They sometimes made two trips to my one to the meadow. While the rest of us took time out between loads, they spread fodder for the whole colony, wove garners, or cleaned their shared quarters. They no doubt observed that the meticulous Temerarius kept an immaculate bunker.

A young pair I called Tummy and Gutty may have been too young to have mated for baby pikas. Ordinarily pikas don't mate until they are about two years old. Tummy and Gutty spent much of their time with younger animals whose one motivation appeared to be food. Their garners at the entrance of their bunker were so poorly constructed that I often felt tempted to reweave them for fear the wind would scatter them for miles.

Of all Square Top Mountain pikas, Mama Sapiens stood out as the epitome of intelligence, strength of character, and selflessness. Through Mama Sapiens the colony accepted me—taught me many of its secrets. Apparently an elderly widow of vast experience, she tutored young pikas when they first left their family corridors. As colony matriarch she attempted more than her share in every talus task. She amassed the largest garners. After I knew her better, it seemed reasonable to assume this was in order to help those who would fall into need come winter. Every evening when I left the talus, she performed extra sentry duty—despite dawn-to-dark harvesting. Before long I referred to her in my notes as "the grand old lady of Rock-slideland." Her example suggested that animals, like people, become individuals—moral beings, each with personal beauty and dignity, trustees of love and respect.

Three apprentice harvesters followed Mama Sapiens through every harvest activity. Each of the trio carried his or her share of fodder to the topmost bunkers. A bright little fellow I called Sunny never seemed to tire from reveille till sunset. A very small pika I referred to as Teeny often lay on her belly and rested after a round trip between the talus and meadow; then she would rush down for the next load. Something had happened to the third "apprentice" that had left him with a pronounced handicap, so the one I called Limpy struggled a bit harder than the others in order to carry his share. He was the one pika that seemed to shrink from the hot, dusty winds that now blew more frequently from the Red Desert and parched the hinterland.

Little Miss Humdrum worked as one of Mama Sapiens's understudies, but she lacked the initiative and imagination of her mentor. Miss Humdrum simply plodded. All signs seemed to indicate that she would follow her own tracks day after day until her habitual routines created a visible runway. Such behavior disturbed me, because sooner or later a carnivore would zero in on her rut. In her methodical way she looked up at me and "smiled" from her habitual position near my sleeping bag at predawn reveille. She was so fussy about detail that she invariably sat at Mama Sapiens's right side.

To each of several more I tacked on an identifying name: Pliny, the curious, and his mate, Misty. Cocoa, a feisty female without a mate but with two obstreperous youngsters.

The Rockslideland league functioned efficiently because it encompassed a parish composed for the most part of skilled laymen. Primacy, superiority, and seniority received no billet on the talus. Each adult pika fulfilled his duties as his own leader, as partisan to his own family, as patriot to his colony. All positions were *working* positions; there were no administrators, no supervisors.

On the morning of July 28 the final curtain of nonunderstanding vanished like a meadow mist on a windy summer day. Toughy and Mama Sapiens led me to a large gopher snake who was slithering toward the harvesters on the lower end of the meadow. The entire colony stopped work and crouched on lower talus boulders in order to watch me carry the big wiggly snake across the canyon.

They must have noticed that I never ate lunch; but on that July 28, during the midday rest stop, they brought mouthfuls of fresh meadow fodder to where I sat on the Ponder Rock. I did not pretend to eat any of their gifts for fear they would repeat the performance every day and thus waste time, fodder, and energy needlessly.

Routinely enough, that same afternoon we were cutting mature annuals when a pair of moose walked up the trail, trumpeted squatters' rights, and began to mow the herbage. Not even a grizzly bear living at 10,000 feet above sea level in the Wind River Range had lung capacity, muscular resources, or plain guts adequate to challenge so formidable a pair. After a dozen intimidating snorts, the couple ignored our existence. To allow their intrusion to go uncontested would have resulted in further invasion by their relatives, and the meadow would have suffered depletion within several days. Pikas found moose excreta repulsive. By that time I could look Tatters and the pikas squarely in the eyes and broadcast approval, disapproval, pleasure, friendship, security, or danger. I decided upon a collision course with disaster: a stare-down with the moose. Failure would mean a thunderous charge, deadly goring, and tromping; there were no nearby trees to climb.

Armed with more confidence than good sense, I walked swiftly toward two of the most dangerous wild animals in North America. Both moose raised their heads with open, questioning eyes—the medium for receiving messages. At a distance of about twenty feet I stopped and stared at first one, then the other. I tried to put great volumes of disapproval and danger into my stare. At that moment a violent gust of sand-carrying wind slapped the invaders' faces. The two behemoths plunged back down the trail, apparently unaware of my simultaneous broadcast of terror. It was weeks before another moose showed up on the meadow.

I believe the Little Chief hares did everything in their power to make me understand them. They repeated signals, stances, whistles, ear semaphore flickers, stares, and thumps until I reacted—admittedly not always intelligently. Pantomime, barks, scurry-jumps, and semaphores warned of the weasel. They seemed to believe the fissiped

also posed danger to me. When I reacted favorably to a deliberate attempt at communication, most of the colony responded audibly, almost as if celebrating the event of putting across a message. I wrote down and memorized every combination of signals in order to learn pika "vocabulary."

Once understood, the clarity and simplicity of each completed message elated me. Simplification was the infallible key. My whole body tingled, wonder-struck with admiration for these diminutive mammals who were responsible for my attempting to achieve their level of humility and integrity. Ostensibly, the pikas enjoyed the communication game as much as I did. Toughy may have sensed right away my inability ever to repeat some of their signals—ear semaphores, stances, and jumps—but he seemed to expect me to make myself understood in whistled and several facial exchanges.

Mama Sapiens must have noticed that we reciprocated least while resting on Meditation Tower, most when we worked; but she rarely brought her communications to a complete close. She searched my eyes continuously for the slightest change of mental variation, as if she were attempting at all times to hang onto the wavelength of each frame of my disposition. She detected with uncanny accu-

racy every mood and apparently transmitted accordingly
to the colony. She must have known that the conveyance
of an optical message entailed more than looking another
in the eye and blandly thinking a basic emotion. My own
attempts to convey silent communication involved an out-
put of overt effort frequently far more exhausting than
simple labor, because I also pantomimed every feeling I
tried to express to the colonists. As a matter of record, they
understood most of my instantaneous broadcasts to them,
very few of the slow and deliberate. Also, I must admit,
they understood me at all times far better than I ever understood them. One tangible proof of this poured from
sympathetic stares when I fought hardest against inevitable fatigue toward each evening. They may have been
aware that I was imitating them when I sprawled upon the
rock at sunset when the day's work was done. Even though
they may not have been able to register the colors of sunset, that specific time of day presented a delightful adventure in group relaxation, even though the pikas rarely
seemed to tire.

I came to believe that the most difficult and significant
hurdle to understanding "lower" animal messages stood in
the reception and transmission of impressions infinitely
briefer, simpler, and faster than my human brain had been

accustomed to deal with. When a wedge of teal winged across the gusty sunset one evening, eighteen expressions flashed simultaneously to my eyes and back to the teal in an interval of possibly five wingbeats. The message translated and expanded—*enormously*—into human thought may have been: "That flock of teal should be hidden by now in the cattails." Their message also may have included an allusion to a prowler that caused the teal to take to the air.

It would fall into the category of downright exaggeration to claim that ideas crossed the abysmal gap between man and pika. To my knowledge that never occurred as such. With more spectacular illustrations purposely omitted, the following fourteen examples represent a few typical message-type communications I feel were exchanged between me and the pikas:

1. As seasonal ripening for each plant species progressed, Shiny and Bouncy showed me by exhibiting their cuttings not only which plants to take but also the *maturity level* to select. Mama Sapiens demonstrated that she sniffed each stem to detect the ones that had been befouled with urine. Realizing that the human sense of smell could never approach pika sensitivity, I decided to wash each load in Lagomorph Creek before delivering it to the talus. From that time on, the colony rejected very little from the packrack bundles.

2. From Toughy and Smiley I learned signals that warned of enemy approach. As I continued to throw stones at carnivores, however, many pikas compromised traditional habits and ran to me when enemies skulked, indicating that they understood my position of protector. They also ran to me to communicate cessation of harvest activities when droughty gales made it impractical to continue work.

3. With sharp, continuing bleats, the sentries warned of enemy approach. They continued the sounds until I answered with a whistle similar to the pika "eenk," indicating that I acknowledged their warning. Crusty and Smiley pointed out the safest and most direct route from my camp to their Rockslideland bunkers.

4. The predawn reveille at the sleeping bag clearly substantiated a "thought package." The pikas' ability to appraise the characteristics of another species vital to them and to get messages across the intergeneric vacuum represented perhaps more distant removal from simple instinct than we may realize.

5. The colony accepted what I considered biological sanity in the rest stops at Meditation Tower. They also accepted the sunny refuge for afternoon siesta. Two innovations.

6. Mama Sapiens and several mated couples accompanied me on visits to neighboring families of marmots, ground squirrels, chipmunks, and chickarees. As expected, most rodents to whom I was thus introduced lost any instinctive fear almost at once, and as I walked or crawled among them they became almost as gentle as the pikas.

7. When whistling a specific note, haunching, and patting forepaws produced gifts of man-goodies, Shiny and Bouncy repeated that specific routine for that request only and taught it to other pikas. This bit of conditioning—designed to prove the existence of communication—was later to lead to serious conflict with Marcos Eagle Rock.

8. I taught the pikas a particular night call that I thought might serve should an emergency arise after dark. The alarm demonstrated a minor thought transaction; but I abandoned the notion when at length Temerarius, Tummy, and Bitsy used the same signal day or night.

9. On one occasion I observed the pikas' secret investigation of my evening harmonica concert for the year-

ling bear. The day afterward the entire colony haunched near Meditation Tower when I experimented by playing several tunes. Thereafter they shrieked in unison at midday until I performed. This does not imply that they ever understood or enjoyed music, but rather may have indicated a kind of association imprint that first impressions are supposed to engrave upon the animal mind. Strangely though, if I played or otherwise distracted their noontime meditation the day following a carnivore's kill, they crept from the Ponder Rock and retired to their bunkers. They communicated grief each time a colonist fell victim to a killer.

10. Drummer and Skippy demonstrated scorn for nonworkers, loudly deploring the times I gave nuts, dried fruit, guinea pig food, or hamster treats to Mopish or Cadger. They never voiced similar complaints when I gave the same treats to other pikas.

11. Most colonists reacted to forthright messages in my smile—and sometimes watery eyes—by bouncing, chattering, and drawing physically close. At times they raced through a wild sun dance to celebrate my delivery of an especially rich load of gentian and campanule.

12. I believe that each pika deliberately revealed himself or herself to me in a distinctive manner that caused me to relate with him or her personally.

13. Mama Sapiens and Toughy warned me about poisonous nightshade, monkshood, larkspur, and locoweed by jumping between the sickle and the plant, by shrieking if I tried to include any one of the four in fodder bundles. At times these plants proved difficult to recognize, their flowers having spent themselves on winds of June. But the pikas *always* recognized them.

14. One day five mated pikas led me to a keystone boulder at the foot of the talus and solemnly dramatized through guttural chatter a problem with that particular monolith. They may have noticed a general tremor

throughout the scree when a keystone slipped an inch or two.

In the standard sense of human-evolved language, there existed, or course, no rational dialogue among the pikas themselves that I was ever able to discover. But through optical expression, single-noted phonetics, and body movements, specific meanings had developed to haunting proportions. Perhaps with slight alteration of traditionally defined linguistics, the pikas and I engaged in symbolic dialogue of sorts. We certainly developed an ecstasy of understanding, trust, and collaboration.

Shame and ignorance strapped me the morning Toughy sat comfortably in my cupped palms, looked me straight in the eye, and whispered a fellowship something-or-other that I shall be forever poorer for lack of the ability to comprehend.

Like other wild animals I have known, most colonists received my eager wavelength of empathy. There is no doubt in my mind that they sensed a powerful reaching out to them with every fiber and thought of my being.

For so long as I dealt with them as sensitive, intelligent beings, they responded in kind. But every time they read a doubtful eye—every time I brooded upon the experiment as a possibly distorted translation of reality or sheer flight of fancy—a corresponding change took place in the colony. The mentally acute pikas withdrew almost as a unit. And until each wave of uncertainty passed, I stuck out like a desert island in a jungle of untouchable wildness. In the face of increasing drought, dusty winds, and probable failure of food sources, I fought back daily encroachment of doubt that the project could possibly succeed.

A Land of No Possessions

My pledged obligation to the pika borough overgrew into a reflex of devotion to individual colonists. They drew my attention daily to incidents that resulted in trust and dependence. The association flourished, and an uncomplicated satisfaction sprang from duty fulfilled, knowledge gained. A primitive and lively enchantment surged every time younger pikas—Tummy, Gutty, Peppy, Rally, Limpy—fed in confidence from my hands and followed me about the talus and meadow. On each return to our sun-kindled green, a rippling thrill tingled up and down my spine as the singing horde accompanied me, flowing over uneven masses of boulders like a miniature beige gray mist.

For the duration of my season with them, I experienced none of the premeditated exemption from pressures ordinarily associated with summer mountain sojourns; yet

I had never known genuine delight in the rigid responsibility one assumes for the lives of dependent animals until I discovered how to devote full-time energy to the pikas.

Mama Sapiens, Toughy, and Smiley indicated through daily devotion to harvest that my foreign presence would not diminish their independence. Eagle Rock would surely approve of this—so I thought. From such an attitude I drew my resolution to continue the experiment until the snows of late autumn. While graciously accepting the fruits of my labor and friendly protection, no pika ever repressed his own resources or responsibilities. Expressions scintillated, but never flinched, never begged. Smiling through their eyes, the little folk revealed the two paramount preferences of their persuasion: the land of their choice and their devotion to one another, which I chose to interpret as a revelation of true and unchangeable wildness. They were tame without losing the essentials of wild animals.

In homeland surroundings, pika life style—simple one moment, complicated the next—continued to reveal paradoxes. The annual harvest, for example, may have increased their devotion to land and to one another to a degree achieved during no other season; yet the accelerated activity demanded no end of physical labor, incessant exposure to every predaceous animal in the canyon, and less time for socializing.

Drummer and Temerarius yelled at me when I fed the fat mendicant and the blind Cadger; yet *they* must have fed them in past winters. The colony's morning arrival in camp—even when Tatters sat nearby and gawked—exemplified further paradox for animals reputed to be among the most timid in America.

In the blind pika I sensed a none-too-gentle innuendo, an intimation of what it was like to survive ineffectually the careless moments that had rendered him blind. He may have appeared to enjoy his inactivity; but I could not help feeling that he suffered most while the rest of the colony enjoyed the rigors of harvest activities.

Parent pikas communicated lore to their young, and the teaching blossomed despite almost insuperable odds in that rocky citadel of setbacks, dilemmas, and paradoxes. The immature provided fascinating behavior to observe as they shuffled across the rocks, appearing to select, assort, and reorganize what their parents had taught earlier in the day: camouflage, escape routines, courtesies toward one another, fodder spreading and turning, garner weaving, housekeeping, and ceaseless scrutiny within the vastness of the mountain range.

In the sleeping bag early on the night of July 29, I lay reflecting upon a day well applied. My muscles ached but no longer twitched and cramped after reaping and conveying five loads to the upper talus where changing shifts of pikas took turns spreading and sun curing. I was gradually becoming toughened to my task, broken in to my taskmasters.

Tatters squirmed in helpless, noisy rage as he sat and tapped my head with his paw—threatening to pitch a tantrum, unconvinced that I had unequivocally concluded graham crackers, wrestling, harmonica, and campfireside chin scratching for the evening. He refused to accept heavy eyelids as a justifiable excuse for cancellation of our walk to the lake. In an ursine way of compounding logic, he must have thought that only a fool would try to sleep in such exposing brilliance of moonlight. It was the first time I had seen the moon reach higher than our mountains. To block out the bear's unendurable gaze, I closed my eyes.

At length he trundled away, hungry for wood slugs and serviceberries at the marsh. Soporific stillness lengthened between songs of owl, tree toad, and cricket. The strident creekside choral ensemble chanted sleep time solutions to the perplexing problems of tomorrow, while perpetual orbits of stars suggested that night celebrated the natural triumph of order over the chaos of the human day. I lay there cursing my own weakness and vagrant brain for dismissing Tatters while muted echoes of his tormentors—owls, wolverines, rams, and moose—still lingered in box ravines that dead-ended in cul-de-sacs on both sides of the Green River gorge. I fell asleep partially recognizing, but ignoring, an alarm from the talus.

Ominous silence prevailed in the predawn owllight on July 30. A nervous delegation of fewer pikas than usual zigzagged around the sleeping bag. Distressed expressions clouded their faces. There was no way of knowing how long they had shuttled breathlessly back and forth, a moving diorama of stony-serious lilliputian elfins. Only when satisfied that I had indeed regained consciousness did they scuff through dry leaves and duff with shockingly unexpected voice and movement. There had been an exigency of some kind. Their voices resonated strong hints of trouble, but they would have to lead me to it. I had no way of interpreting the cause of their anxiety.

By midday break we had rounded out three trips to the topmost garners. The pikas kept trying to communicate something. There was a moment when I believed I had the answer. A number of garners had disappeared. Presumably the colonists had taken the cured "hay" into their bunkers for storage. I had not been overconcerned with what they did with the fodder I delivered once the sun had cured it.

I scanned the talus repeatedly through binoculars, but observed nothing else out of order. No one was missing, yet they jabbered at me from all sides—and shrieked at one another—as we trudged up and down the slope. Scotty babbled so much she dropped the stems she was carrying, but she chattered on, for the first time ignoring lost fodder. Returning to the meadow for the fourth load, Mama Sapiens and Toughy became even more garrulous. Their eyes bulged as if some scandal or threatening mystery skulked about Rockslideland. At least I had made the progress necessary to recognize anxiety in the colony's behavior.

Centuries of vigilance had rendered pikas pop-eyed. The resulting wide-angled vision, especially among those who had served many seasons as sentinels, was well suited for locating peripheral movement of eagles, owls, and hawks. On that particular day their eyes all but stuck out on stems. We sunned ourselves on the Ponder Rock when the fourth load had been spread. After studying an emboldened coyote 600 feet below, I arced a stone. Smiley pounced his supple little body onto my lap. Toughy, Skippy, Mousey, Crusty, and the two potbellied youngsters, Tummy and Gutty, followed suit almost as if they had drilled the maneuver. They had also observed the distant prowler. But something deeper gnawed at their minds—a message I failed to fathom even partially. I still thought it strange that I had not seen them dismantle the intricately woven garners, but I assumed they had done the work after I had gone to sleep.

With an unintentional outburst of laughter at a scuffle among the colonists jockeying for lap positions, I recalled that one of Gulliver's articles of agreement forbade him ever to handle a lilliputian without the subject's consent. I laughed at a sudden figment of imagination: Lemuel Gulliver was none other than Jonathan Swift; the lilliputians were pikas! It was enough to make a person believe in reincarnation.

I sat dreading the thought of what might happen to our pleasant relationship should another human being intrude upon that rocky canton, when forthwith the dark outline of a man appeared about 500 yards below us. He stood motionless at the side of a saddled horse on the trail

between our meadow and the marsh immediately upstream above Green River Lake. He had focused binoculars in the direction of Meditation Tower. I waved. He
mounted, then waved back casually. Mousey and Drummer fired six rapid "eenks." Every pika shot from the Ponder Rock and disappeared into deep corridors below the
surface boulders. They too had sighted the intruder.

Shouldering the packframe, I climbed down toward
the horseman, who now advanced along the lower end of
the Lagomorph Creek meadow.

It wasn't exactly surprising to see Eagle Rock ride up
the trail. He dismounted, replaced his binoculars in a saddlebag, and fidgeted with the old mustang's reins. Something annoyed him. We shook hands and exchanged
amenities.

"Your relationship with the Little Chiefs is all wrong,
Bob," he said in muffled tones as if concealing his words
from a steadily approaching tide of pikas. "I have studied
your actions and attitude through binoculars."

After careful reconnaissance, the pikas no doubt recognized the Amerind and advanced eagerly. Although
they were little more than squirming shadows at our feet, I
sensed that they were attempting to communicate with the
shaman as they had been trying to make me understand
them all day.

"Everywhere you have interfered with the Little
Chiefs' true nature, they will suffer. This very trail repre-
sents man's interference with Green River wildlife. All
man-made trails subvert nature because all animals now
use them. Predators and hunters also use them, a conve-
nient way to take an unnatural number of prey species,
which upsets native balance."

He spoke to me but his eyes remained fixed upon the
pikas. Perhaps he was unaware that the US Forest Service
trail followed a natural game path between the Green
River and Pine Creek watersheds.

"I have changed nothing in the lives of your Little Chiefs," I assured him. "I may have tamed them too much, but I have done only what you asked me to do. They refused to cooperate until I became almost one of them."

"You have been standing guard over them. They have their own sentinels. If man guards them, they will learn to sleep in the sun . . . hawks will stoop from the cliffhead. Fox, weasel, marten, skunk will know when man also sleeps in the sun. What the hell *is* this business? Sitting on a rock and laughing when there's a harvest that won't wait to be gathered! I watched you for an hour. The coyote is now bolder because he sees you pampering the Little Chiefs. He has communicated with his kind that you are unarmed, that you throw stones, not bullets. You gave me your word you would alter nothing here. This alpine zone is the most delicate of all life zones. A careless person can sometimes inflict irreparable damage just by walking over it."

He continued to study Mama Sapiens, Toughy, and Smiley. He wrapped the reins of his horse around his forefinger. In my own mind I knew that he had experienced much deeper subtleties with pikas than I had. He had plumbed their depths more profoundly through many years of study and native affinity; like other Amerinds, he had scrupulously avoided precipitating environmental crises. He reflected inherent racial insight into ecological integrity.

"Devotion to their own kind—not to an outsider— makes them strong," he continued, shaking an accusing finger and looking me in the eye. "Perpetual struggle. If you stay, they cannot survive. You must leave today."

"The harvest is not a tenth part in. No! I will not leave till frost. I've grown to love the pikas very dearly. I'll see it through and without harm to your Little Chiefs. I've kept my agreement to the letter."

"You've lost position and so have they. Your *love* for

the Little Chief reeks of fascination. Curiosity. Maybe charity. Not love. The way you are handling it, their harvest cannot succeed before frost. They will do better on their own."

"My only consideration is the pikas' welfare. How would you have done it differently?"

"Your job was to fill the bunkers with meadow herbs and grasses. You weren't supposed to tame the pikas! What you have done could bring about their annihilation." He looked down at the swarm around our feet. "You don't understand our Earth Mother. Your blood is only *part* Indian. You have overstepped into the Shoshonean world, which is *all* Indian."

A bit of heat rose around the nape of my neck. He probably guessed that the colonists were teaching me more of their communication system than he wanted me to know. To him, pika knowledge was to remain a secret of the Shoshone shaman. I retorted more forcefully than good manners would have dictated.

"I recognize my own deficiencies, Eagle Rock, but did you think an ecologist could come up here without getting personally involved with the wildlife?"

"Ecologists misinterpret the Great Spirit."

"From what I've seen, your Great Spirit is on vacation. While Gitche Manito sleeps, your devil spirits work. I've watched the carnivores hone their appetites. And what about this goddamned drought? Can your Great Spirit do something about that?"

"Leave!" He stood as straight as a lodgepole. Outraged. But he did not raise his voice.

"I will *not* leave until the work is done. This land is not Shoshone!" I was ashamed of myself for shouting. "It's *public* land. These animals don't belong to the Shoshone. Your anger is an admission that your Little Chiefs have shown me what you thought was exclusively yours."

"Bob, you are trying to cultivate orchids where only

cacti grow." He lowered his voice and dropped his hands to his sides. "By now you should have gathered more than half the harvest. And why haven't you? Because you daydream on your fanny in the sunshine and tame the Little Chiefs on your lap. Because you are trying to learn what you can *never* learn. Because you waste time stoning predators. These hills also belong to the predator."

"Are pikas serfs to a particular talus that rocks back and forth on a shaky foundation?" I demanded. "Why haven't you moved this colony to safer quarters with more plentiful pasture if they mean so much to you? Because you're utterly hidebound, that's why."

"To them their land is worth all its work, pain, drought, and frost. They would accept no disengagement from this, their world. Physical and moral toughness guarantees survival—not taming and pampering."

Instead of turning away as I expected, he rambled on about the Earth Mother and why the white man disregarded Amerind law, but I no longer listened.

"Natural law," he said, "excludes human right either to question, command, or persuade."

"Your words are baked air. They tumble to the granite," I said. "There is no alternative to resolve the conflict between us."

He was too angry to reason with. Even if his anger cooled, he would never agree to my tie-in with the colony, which he had carefully appraised through binoculars long before I knew he was in the vicinity. More inflexible and intolerant than most men of his experience, he was at the same time far more sensitive to the total alpine ecosystem than I could ever be. According to his indictment, my guilt lay in a serious violation of Amerind law. I had stoned a coyote, consequently interfering with natural balance. I had gone beyond his expectations in an attempt to span a gap between species. In my own conscience I felt that I had challenged none of his ecological gospel, none of the naked authenticity of Amerind law to which I subscribed the same as he. Our conflict appeared to have arisen exclusively from my intimate personal accomplishment in such a short time with his colony. He feared the final extent to which I might go. It shocked, frightened, and—in his eyes—deprived him of what he thought should remain exclusively Shoshone.

Except for a moment of indecision, I almost succumbed to the temptation to pack my rucksack and leave. Regrettable fury almost choked me before I regained composure.

"Time, Marcos Eagle Rock, is the highest price we pay for anything. I'm devoting full time to this project. Without man's help now, the colony cannot survive the winter. I'll leave only if you take over. Otherwise, I stay till frost."

His eyes registered no more emotion than if he had not heard my words. He had seen how the pikas had accepted me, but he must have known I could penetrate little beyond a thin outer rind in correspondence with them. Furthermore, he knew he could depend upon it that without a hundred years at least in which to catch up with Shoshone lore, I would hardly scratch the surface of his secrets. But the mere fact that I had launched an arrow toward a tribal arcanum stunned him with resentment.

"I apologize, Marc, for my anger. But I won't leave unless I have your word you will stay."

"You know I cannot." He handed me the reins of his horse, walked slowly to the center of the meadow, withdrew a buckskin pouch from beneath his denim shirt, sprinkled corn pollen toward the four cardinal directions, and spoke in his native dialect.

The witch doctor's entreaty. The corn pollen invocation was never recited except as an appeal for powerful leverage. In English I heard him address something to "Lightning, Son of Fire. . . ." I assumed he was praying for lightning to strike me dead before I could further desecrate his Little Chiefs. The same invocation, however, could have indicated a prayer for rain.

He returned to his horse, mounted, and looked toward the talus. The pikas slowly seethed about my feet, scratching and slipping as they tried to climb the legs of my jeans. Their eyes clinched with the shaman's face. Rigidly Eagle Rock turned and spoke to me. Rancor quivered in his shaky voice.

"Squirrels have invaded and taken many garners along the northwest ridge. Now that you have stoned the predators, rodents make mockery of your work and rape the Little Chiefs' winter supplies. See if you can somehow make up the loss."

Shamans engage in no fly-by-night convictions. They embrace the moral sophistication and time-tested philosophy of the Ancient Ones. Marc was no exception.

I hated to see him leave in anger, believing that I had shirked my duty and jeopardized his Little Chiefs. By the time he headed back down the trail, it was too late to climb the northwest ridge for assessment of rodent pillage. In order somewhat to mollify a rasping conscience, I cut and delivered one more load of fodder for south ridge dwellers. Aware of my simmering anger, the pikas stared at me constantly, but maintained total silence until I returned to camp. I had forgotten about the sunset ritual at the Ponder Rock.

Nighttime worry was gradually draining away my stamina. Among other gall-coated Square Top Mountain truths, it became evident that I could no longer take pika troubles to the sleeping bag and retain sanity at work the next day. I might as well try to sleep with a fully loaded packrack and rucksack strapped to my back. Each day's task demanded a night of untroubled rest; therefore, I resolved stubbornly to shut out Marcos Eagle Rock and his Little Chiefs' burdens between sunset and the time the little horde's eyes "shouted" reveille. Circumstantial factors within their fragile domain rose and fell with such regularity anyway that I rather expected extensive fluctuations from night to day. Sleeptime worry only impaired intelligent solutions and availed nothing.

But squirrels! There weren't that many at 10,000 feet above sea level. Why had Toughy, Shiny, and Temerarius permitted a theft without a fight? Also of lively significance, the colonists had tried all day, ineffectually, to relay news of the adversity; and that bothered me because on numerous occasions they had successfully conveyed more complicated messages. They had neglected to lead me to an example of their loss, yet they had led me to a loose boulder that frightened them. There was no doubt about it, most essential channels to eye talk still eluded me.

Eagle Rock had not set foot on the talus. Yet he knew about the pillaging rodents. Could they have imparted such a complex communication to him? There had to be another explanation.

It seemed at the time that losses due to squirrels further justified man's help in time of pika need. I could find nothing destructive in that idea. My own commitment demanded that I violate no natural laws—often distasteful laws to the human mind (but that did not mean they were consequently evil laws). With extreme caution I told myself that man might help a troubled wildling and in the bargain further his own self-realization without upsetting wilderness codes—a forthright belief but somewhat opposed to Eagle Rock's principle of "hands off, man."

Stingy Pasture

By sunrise on the morning of July 31, the colony and I had appraised our losses. Because northwest ridge pikas had woven many garners into crevices slightly below surface boulders along the lower quadrants, it proved extremely difficult for me to estimate accurately the amount of cured fodder the squirrels had plundered. It looked as if about half the pika supplies were missing.

The gyrfalcon provided a key to the location of the thieves' dens where she rose from the canyon with a taloned squirrel. With packrack shouldered, I descended along a little-used game trail that led directly to the robbers' encampment. The pikas refused to follow. Sure enough, the falcon had observed while the rodents constructed secret stacks of woven twigs—like inverted eagles' nests—along the brushy right bank of a dry wash fifty yards below the talus toward upper Green River Lake.

Unlike pikas, squirrels hibernated; but they did not begin the deep sleep until December, a month after the last available food lay out of reach under twenty feet of snow. In the meantime, they had to eat; so they warehoused food. The first rick I tore apart yielded a half bushel of pika fodder and one terrified squirrel family unwilling to defend either the loot or the den they had built for hibernation. By evening I had dislodged sixteen families and returned eight loads of provender to the talus.

In the auraglow of sunset I chanced upon two intelligent reasons why the pikas had declined to follow and help me redeem their hay. At dusk the squirrels, determined to reacquire the fragrant fodder I had hauled away, headed once again for Rockslideland. As a godsend for the pikas, but calamity for the rodents, a veritable squadron of owls, having also observed the squirrel industry during the past several days, congregated almost as if some local advocate had passed "word" around that a windfall of warm flesh would venture forth on that particular evening. And that accounted for the first reason the pikas had refused to help; they feared raptors would arrive, but did not know precisely when.

Had I known more about rodents, I would have recognized that squirrels, in order to ensure retention of booty, rarely seized or stored anything as food without first bestowing upon it the scent of their urine, surest way in the wild to keep fastidious pikas from reclaiming their own— or even fighting to hold it once the squirrels had touched it.

When recovery finally reached completion, I had stacked about 150 pounds of repossessed fodder against the cliff for purification in sun-simmered air, hoping the pikas would tolerate a faintly restricting essence of squirrel urine come winter's hard truths of starvation. I could not be certain that rain or soaking in the creek would improve it in the pikas' eyes.

That evening as we sat on the tower, I decided, in light of the time factor and the continuing drought that had begun to take a dreadful toll, to foil predation and pilferage wherever the pikas were concerned—and to hell with Eagle Rock and his principle. All evidence at hand now indicated that nothing short of a miracle at Square Top Mountain could get the pikas through the long winter ahead. With my legs swinging over the edge of the boulder, I spat repeatedly into space and contemplated the so-called balanced ecosystem, another paradox in Cragrockland. Correctly stated, perfectly balanced ecosystems do not exist.

Reality (as indicated by the age of several squirrel lodges) suggested that pack rats and squirrels had *always* plundered *Ochotona* garners on tali that bordered rodent territory. Eagle Rock would have known this. Like other adversities, the theft had probably bolstered colony unity. The Shoshone had indicated in bold capitals that my *negligence* had contributed to a loss that in fact had transpired annually for ages—albeit perhaps less serious in normal years when weather signs pointed to much later frost. There was also an outside possibility that the shaman had learned of the theft simply by observing squirrel activities on his way up the canyon trail. Even if he knew of prior raids on pika supplies by rodents, he was not de facto guilty of deliberate dishonesty. In his opinion my vigilance should have been sufficiently sharp to preclude loss of any kind without his having to mention the possibility ahead of time. He was no doubt disappointed in his prior presumption that I would be able to perform miracles since I had been sent—according to his thinking—by the spirit of Sacajawea.

"Tamed and pampered!" he had exclaimed. "Physical and moral toughness!"

One of Eagle Rock's criticisms rightfully piqued my conscience: By the end of July, local fauna had lost fear of me. Carnivores and gatherers alike had suffered outrages at the triggers of the gunpowder set in a variety of painful tragedies; but I tossed relatively harmless rocks that barely startled and didn't even hurt in the rare event of contact. Timid bighorn sheep from lofty crags along the divide had watched me sit, eat, wrestle, and walk night after night with a black bear—an assiduously hunted big game animal. The tattered yearling showed not the remotest fear of the rock thrower. An entire canyon population had witnessed dawn-to-dark companionship with the pikas—had seen them crawl all over me with impunity. Chipmunks, marmots, porcupines, hares, and birds paraded regularly through camp for hand-held tidbits. Hence my status in the wildlife mind frightened me. An imminent Bridger National Forest hunting season would wreak tragedy upon game species because of my gentling influence. Eagle Rock's denunciation upbraided my conscience day and night, yet I was unable to alter my habits—fully realizing possible consequences. It was exactly like trying to kick an addiction.

Increasing warmth of affection extended by the colonists no doubt caused me to magnify their natural afflictions, which at times may have bordered upon the trifling. When I found Gutty and Tummy vomiting near their quarters, I dropped the packrack, scooped them up to my lap, and imagined an epidemic about to break out. Toughy brought me the chewed remains of a plastic sack that had contained my homemade granola. No damage done. But the shock taught a good lesson.

Because of an insane rush to recoup the fodder stolen by the squirrels, I painfully twisted an ankle, cut an arm, bruised both knees, barked the fingers of my right hand, and tore my clothing. Thanks to extravagant sharing with Tatters, my food supply rapidly dwindled and disappeared; so I had to hike to the station wagon and back—about sixteen miles—for replenishment at a time when an accumulation of ailments made the journey downright miserable.

Hobbling back up the trail on the wrenched ankle, I realized how easily men resolved their food and shelter problems compared with the pikas. Picturing arctic gales howling among glacial drifts at fifty below zero, I stopped cursing my short inventory of inconveniences.

Inevitably an advancing season stole away the hours with unrelenting speed. Taking into account the shaman's visit, escalating predation, lack of normal rainfall, rodent damage to the garners, and the end of man-fear among local carnivores, I gave up the last lingering interest in scientific observation of wildlife for that year. Time became too precious to squander on objectivity. Toward the end of each twelve hours of rock and harvest, I merely wished to feel that I had performed in the pikas' best interest.

The little gnomes went about renewing their garners as if the humiliating theft had never happened. With exemplary work habits, Mama Sapiens, Toughy, Smiley, and Bouncy quickly reinspired enthusiasm among dwellers on the northwest ridge. In order to offset their losses, I delivered extra loads to the ridge. Pikas living on the south slope probably understood. No one voiced an "eenk" of objection.

On occasion I took a small sack of oatmeal or a package of raisins to Meditation Tower. As much as the colonists delighted in these rare goodies, they never intercepted, scrambled, or scuffled to receive the treats. Had I not pressed for equal sharing, the bucks would have stepped aside and allowed the does and young to have the entire amount. On the other hand—and this is not unique among colony animals—Skippy, Bouncy, Bitsy, and Spot invariably shared oatmeal, nuts, raisins, granola, and hamster treats with their mates whether or not I did the rationing. While division was not always equal, these animals had learned self-mastery to an amazing degree; they enjoyed the most effective government on Earth: self-control under all circumstances. Eons ago necessity had taught that selfishness ranked as number one depravity, capable of enfeebling a colony more effectively than any combination of earthly calamities. So, as a natural function within character, they shared, as civilized man shares with less fortunate brethren.

For the Square Top Mountain pikas, granola was a detour into pure luxury. A preparation of roasted nuts, oatmeal, crushed corn flakes, soybean flour, puffed rice, shredded coconut, wheat germ, raisins, and brown sugar that distance hikers concocted, it was not actually called granola in those days. Someone had christened the old standby *trailmate*. Backpackers in the know preferred trailmate to pemmican, K-rations, or dehydrateds. Light to carry, tasty, inexpensive, nutritious, and of high caloric value, the mixture still appeals to mountaineers. To the pikas, granola represented a sensual indulgence for which they had learned to express a special signal of communication: a haunch with chattering teeth or a whistle, patting forepaws, and optical expression that left no doubt. How quickly they learned! And I suffered mild ecoguilt.

In all probability, the survival of the Little Chief society depended less upon ability than upon zeal. Although endowed with ample intelligence, Toughy, Shiny, and Drummer displayed little external evidence of superior prowess. They never cut and trimmed harvested stems to six-inch lengths on the meadow before transporting the fodder to their quarters. Hauling uncut, untrimmed branches entailed half again as much labor because of parts discarded at the time of spreading and curing. After two dozen attempts, I gave up trying to teach efficiency. The otherwise astute Mama Sapiens always attempted more than she could accomplish: filling garners; overseeing Peppy, Rally, Tummy, Gutty, and Limpy; standing sentry duty until all Rockslideland slept; teaching a less-than-brilliant two-legger to communicate. Temerarius, in order to travel his route between the meadow and his hermitage in a straight line, climbed and descended an unnecessary number of huge boulders. The pika suffered no loss, however, despite his man-deplored extravagances.

Another folly appeared in a digression from natural law: compromise. Eagle Rock no doubt recognized this crack in their tough outer shell. When Peppy, Rally, Tummy, and Gutty saw me chuck a stone at a coyote, or when venal crows swooping down ostentatiously, led a fox to outer-perimeter bunkers, the younger pikas *ran to me*. A compromise.

Further examples illustrated concession. Northwest ridge families yielded to the squirrels without a fight; others conceded feeding rights to rodents on the meadow. Toughy, Shiny, and Mousey ran from the weasel (usually) instead of ganging up against him. As a temporal society, their cavalier attitude toward *now* proved a dangerous compromise. I was to observe a long list of compromises before I left Cragrockland.

* * *

For all practical purposes the Wind River Range year included but two seasons: spring and winter. During the spring and perhaps the six weeks of "autumn" that followed before freeze-up, the pikas had to accomplish a year's work and avoid seasonal concentration of misfortunes as much as possible. Heightening activity, Red Desert windstorms, and nippy nights at the end of July whetted carnivore appetites. From the beginning of August, the pika sentinels and I doubled our vigilance.

As if to complement existing hazards, one skulking pair of foxes with an earlier memory of succulent pika

flesh practiced a lethal maneuver on August 2. When hunting, two cooperating foxes were more effective than four working alone. A dog fox passed near enough to drive a pika into a bunker, but he kept on running down the slope. The vixen, who followed at a short distance, then crouched—sun at her back—over the opening where the prey had disappeared. When the pika peeped out and saw the first fox far down the talus, he emerged. Foxes, true sons and daughters of life-through-wits, either made their maneuvers succeed or changed their strategy.

Throughout the last days of the harvest season, possibly as a result of the prolonged drought, fearsome alliances of unrelated species established several new hunting practices with frightful success. During a rest stop on the Ponder Rock on August 3, Crusty and Spot pointed our attention toward a pair of peregrine falcons that led the gyrfalcon to an ailing goose on a beach of the upper lake. The gyr made the kill, took what she and her tercel wanted, then allowed the peregrine pair to pick the carcass. That same afternoon Toughy and Skippy focused their stares on a marten that had blocked a marmot's den on an upper brae until a coyote arrived to dig out the victim. The two fissipeds then sparred for several rounds to settle the issue of who should receive the choicest "cuts" of the marmot. At sunset ravens circled a hiding fawn until a pair of bobcats reached the site. The scavenger birds relished viscera a bobcat wouldn't touch. On one occasion we saw a weasel summon a skunk to the upper meadow when he met the big gopher snake that had returned after I had packed him away. A quartet of crows signaled the cougar when a flock of bighorns outdistanced a limping ewe. Such events the pikas and I witnessed with increasing alarm as the catastrophic drought dragged on.

As we harvested, I watched for fresh examples of group behavior among the pikas. As with most colony animals, families agreed upon specific areas for cluster work.

Toughy and Skippy, Shiny and Bouncy were "next-door" neighbors and therefore mowed and garnered together. Smiley, Bitsy, Mousey, and Scotty did the same. However, when Crusty and Spot fell behind in their quotas, Mama Sapiens, Miss Humdrum, and Limpy distributed the fruits of their labor until the older pair had garnered equal provisions. Occasionally Toughy, Temerarius, Crusty, and the younger bucks ganged up to drive nonresident hares, pack rats, and voles from the meadow. During August, Crusty began to slow down. Twice I stoned a weasel from the vicinity of his and Spot's bunker.

Each pika knew he could trust his pika neighbor. Although mated pairs lived and worked together for life, they conceived and executed most tasks as colony projects. Community cooperation exceeded anything I had ever seen outside the insect world. As blood relatives, individuals looked essentially alike, yet strong differences set personalities apart. Toughy and Skippy shared everything—even granola—with other pikas. Mousey and Scotty served the colony both as sentries and as reapers of huge food stores. Smiley graciously stepped aside when others crowded in. Toughy inclined to elbow his way through a gathering, but I formed a distinct impression that he acted to break up assemblies that might invite hawks and owls.

From the first day of my mission, I observed Toughy cutting and trimming forage and stacking it to one side in order that other pikas might take it to their garners. To me there was never an obvious way to determine who the recipients would be, but he no doubt kept a mental list of those entitled to the help.

With but the exceptions of Mopish and Temerarius, allegiance to colony, family, and self prevailed in that order. Although families and single pikas enjoyed complete autonomy, there appeared to be stronger adherence to tribe than to self. The pikas dazzled human imagination by *loyalty* to their establishment rather than dependence upon it or rejection of it.

Badgering elements, varieties and numbers of enemies, poverty of pasture, and relentless competitors for forage kept the families of every Wind River species small. Further to intimidate the pikas, so it seemed, their cherished talus itself rumbled—a fragile homeland whose brittleness crackled throughout hollow spaces far beneath the surface. Every margin of miscalculation provided a shortcut to extinction. Necessity dictated the crucial choices; yet those very choices seemed infernally ringed with either compromise or misfortune.

By choice the families "meditated" through a siesta hour; by choice they enjoyed the harvest labor; by choice they demonstrated prudence and restraint in the face of nature's waste and improvidence. I watched a pair I called Shiny and Bouncy. It was their youngster that the vixen had tricked on August 2. Although profound grief momentarily desolated them, they bore the adversity with equanimity and returned to routine work the following day, a blue Monday for all of us.

Outwardly an uncomplicated species, the pikas' visible simplicity often camouflaged subtleties in several aspects of their lives. While Bouncy flitted about the meadow apparently accomplishing nothing each morning before her compeers began work, I discovered that she was scouting the area for lurking snakes. Smiley appeared to be the best-natured animal on the hill. The normal anxieties of a pika's day never really upset him. This important individual in fact arbitrated territorial claims on the meadow for pikas, marmots, ground squirrels, and field mice. Pikas preferred compromise to the uncertain outcome of a fight. When not baby-sitting, Crusty and Spot worked as trimmers, spreaders, and dryers of the harvest and acted as decoys along the northwest ridge of the settlement. On four occasions the pursued pair trumpeted to alert me of their approach as they lured fox, marten, weasel, and coyote within range of my rock-throwing arm.

In no case did I ever see a pika engage in bluff tactics. When Toughy, Smiley, Shiny, Mousey, Crusty, and Mama Sapiens formed a phalanx on the morning of August 5 and drove a forty-pound beaver from their meadow, the group action—without casualty—must have reflected the self-knowledge each participant commanded; otherwise, they would never have undertaken the job. The eviction, from plan to execution, could have achieved success only as the result of responsibility to the team by each one-pound dynamo.

Dignity and tenacity distinguished most does in that quaint little Switzerland of the mountainside. Instinctively they learned and practiced self-reliance; but no female pretended self-sufficiency. Therefore, no doe ever fancied it beneath her dignity to accept help in emergencies. Throughout their windblown commonwealth, Temerarius alone flaunted himself as a symbol of pika independence.

Mama Sapiens, whom I assumed to be a self-reliant widow, supervised maturing pikas (a communal activity). She often took it upon herself to drive squatter rodents from the talus, leaving Smiley again faced with an arbitration powwow. Mousey, a somewhat timid male—though a dependable performer in group activitites—on that same August 5 "eenked" at my feet until I followed him to a teasel moorland on a shelf immediately south of the talus. Here stood a fine reserve of ungrazed fodder. Should the meadow prove inadequate or deteriorate from overgrazing and the lack of rain, the reserve was close enough for practical harvest. Other pikas also shifted from their type roles in order to perform extraordinary services to the colony. I saw Peppy, Rally, and Scotty leading a group of young bucks one day. They dashed about from spread to spread in order to help carry curing provender into the owners' bunkers when sudden, high-velocity wind threatened to blow the stores away. Every time an owl or hawk soared, Crusty and Spot called Rally, Gutty, Drummer, and Peppy, all of whom raced about as extra decoys to confuse the raptor and thus serve the general welfare.

It shakes human complacency that pikas so long ago learned that social control functioned best when founded not upon the dominance of an alpha fellow creature, but upon customs that could be respected by the entire colony. Perhaps because their land afforded so little, there were no profitable temptations to breed rogues.

Wilderness life never implies a mere biological inventory of species that make up a local flora and fauna. It manifests a living web—savage, loving, and frequently magnificent. Thus, on that sultry afternoon when eight members of a neighboring pika colony from a canyon slope farther south appeared on our meadow, nearby observers may have intuited that the Little Chiefs of Rockslideland would shortly uncork speedy devices of destruction. The blue jay sounded as if he had ruptured his vocal cords in making the announcement, while expectations among gaping carnivores caused salivary glands to pump. With pinion tips fingering a thermal updraft, a pair of vultures wheeled their shadows around and around the meadow, gambling a little time against what they considered an inevitable battle. War within a species is always far deadlier than any intergeneric fight.

An Epidemic of Lethargy

When no fight developed, the vultures gave up waiting. They flew off in the direction of the Green River Valley and were not seen again in Rockslideland.

My knowledge of the pika's inner world increased somewhat when the visiting delegation of eight strangers scurried across the meadow for a rip-snorting rigadoon of interpersonal play. Some were quiet for short intervals, but shifting eyes and feet betrayed hilarious internal levity. At a discreet distance I clung to the scene with binoculars.

When the neighboring folk finally departed, each carrying a sprig of fodder, they headed back toward their slopeland 500 yards upstream. An adult council appeared to have selected four of our puling youngsters to leave with them. Four of theirs remained on our meadow. Mama

Sapiens brought the newcomers to where I sat. They fled in terror to the talus.

Apparently for generations Green River pika colonies had affiliated with one another's settlements for the biological sanity of exogamous (not closely akin) mating. And thus I realized, insofar as it was possible for me to comprehend in their terms, how frustrating to them my inability to understand certain details of their communication system must have been.

Once they settled the exogamous exchange issue, hard labor and fresh experiences glutted harvesttide. Assisted by Mama Sapiens and a natural capacity for absorbing abuse, the young exchange recruits seemed to accept Square Top austerity and struggle almost immediately. The old doe taught them constantly to stuff little tufts of grass and sedge throughout the bunkers—bonus tidbits when winter storms prevented access to the garners. Within a week the newcomers joined in the regular harvest treadmill, but they were much longer in accepting the presence of a human helper.

Nature would have rebelled had I envisioned my role as one of custodian. Regardless of personal involvement, I never lost sight of my paramount function: harvest worker. It was *they* who chose to host the outsider. And as many speechless creatures will do, they tried to instill their own ways in the guest. By example, Toughy and Miss Humdrum constantly held up the pattern of work routines. Mama Sapiens always seemed to be demonstrating pika sign language for me. Smiley and Spot appeared to show me a new dimension in devotion. Temerarius stood his ground for independence. Scotty exemplified thrift by collecting what other pikas dropped. One could follow with tactical ease their physical exteriors; but I remained hard-pressed to fathom many deceptively simple-appearing examples of interior fortitude. What, for instance, was behind the instinct that subordinated them to a timetable that induced them in the first place to accept a Gulliver to aid with their harvest? How could they be certain of early frost?

If I broke a routine I had learned from their habits, methods, or routes, they became immediately disturbed, dropping what they were carrying, shrieking, and running in circles. They resumed normal harvesting when I again followed the methods they understood.

Specific survival, I discovered, often lay in trained wildness when violence was merely suspected on the prowl across slopeland. Fate always hoodwinked the foolish, and accidents did happen to the best trained—even to those under my immediate surveillance.

Toughy, Shiny, Smiley, and Mousey—along with their mates—wasted no time in fear of predation as long as carnivores kept out of sight. By and large, *Ochotona* was not foolish enough to live by the lessons of miserable experiences alone—or wise enough to know that adversity often cleared the path to self-preservation. From the Ponder Rock on the afternoon of August 6 we observed a youngster who ignored his training—who slept in the sun, then preened himself alone on a distant boulder while the rest of the colony agonized. At length we saw the goshawk stoop, close, and transport the disdainful one.

Notwithstanding duress of time and environmental misfortunes, including the worst drought on record and losses to predators, Square Top Mountain pikas for the most part sang as they jogged in front of me to and from the meadow. Not as people sing—nevertheless, they *sang*. Melancholy from losses never gnawed into a family long enough for members to succumb to its corrosion. While happy consistency may have dulled their lives a bit, it sharpened their chances of reaching old age. When Toughy, Skippy, and their neighbors indulged in banquets of gooseberries, spiny eglantine, and bitterroot, I wondered if perhaps they relished adversity. Mousey and Scotty may have sung happily in the knowledge that although harshness never diminished in Cragrockland, it changed form from time to time.

Late on the afternoon of August 7, Temerarius, the hermit, from his rocky lair at the very top of the talus, sirened the first alarm. I lay draped out in Ponder Rock sunshine between dray loads. The sun had long passed meridian, and most pikas sprawled on the shady sides of nearby boulders, refugees from the muggy heat reflecting from shiny black surfaces. Temerarius's unmistakable signal, however, flagged everyone to attention. To illustrate their consistency in vigilance, Mama Sapiens, Toughy, and Peppy summoned my attention to a miragelike horse and rider that crept along the trail in an updraft between two unstable air currents of different temperatures and densities produced by greenery on one side of the canyon and black rock talus on the other.

In stony silence, unmindful of the thick, gaseous heat, a distorted Eagle Rock rode a piebald mustang up the path. The unsubstantial air quivered under heat waves and gave the impression that the shaman and his horse were floating over the shimmering, watery pathway along the tilted canyon floor. The phenomenon simply meant that Eagle Rock was prowling in the vicinity and that the trail and the two conflicting air currents happened to parallel at that specific time. The shaman was no doubt still checking the progress of the harvest. I was hoping the pikas and I were also filmy and distorted during those moments. The colonists maintained rocklike stillness as they followed the slow, gauzy movement with their eyes. Within a few minutes a downdraft from the minarets along the divide caused the dissolution of the two currents. The incident supported the precaution that even mirages in the Wind Rivers might prove dangerous. Through binoculars I watched the slender Shoshone and his horse inch up the trail toward Green River Pass. Unfortunately, he had seen me loafing again on the rock with the pikas. In his distorted facial expression I saw that the old gentleman was too infuriated to stop, despite his long trip into the mountains. Perhaps he had seen my siesta through binoculars and interpreted it as a further taming of the pikas.

As we descended for the last load that afternoon, we caught a glimpse of bighorn ewes with lambs trotting toward the meadow's upper slope. The pikas surrounded me and hurled volleys of high-pitched complaints. Their eyes smoldered with rage as they "eenked." Suddenly recalling that pikas would not harvest fodder befouled with excreta—that in their eyes my responsibility was to hurl rocks at *all* invaders, carnivores and otherwise—I almost chased the sheep away. We saw them urinate and defecate on our pasture. But sheep had manured that meadow soil for ages; hence, I decided to suffer the tongues of fifteen outraged pikas and to uphold the Eagle Rock principle. For the rest of that day, neither by eye nor by gesture could I pacify the questioning countenances that stared me down.

A capacity for responsibility peculiarly theirs had elevated the pikas to a high plane without necessarily involving reason. Youthfully abandoning for a time their habitual practice of vigilance, Gutty, Tummy, Rally, and Peppy began romping with the four new pikas. Simultaneously all five sentries trumpeted a danger signal. The eight youngsters haunched and froze, hypnotized in full view of an approaching weasel. Instantly aware of impending tragedy, Toughy, Shiny, Smiley, Mousey, and Mama Sapiens dropped their harvested stems and rushed wide-mouthed toward the carnivore even before I had appraised the emergency. Outflanked, the weasel retreated into the forest. Even though many colonists often engaged in dangerous distractions, there were always those whose native responsibility through wildness warned when danger prowled.

I strongly suspect that the Little Chief hares may have acquired much of their unity as a result of sunny afternoon reflections atop Meditation Tower ages before I took credit for the "innovation." On the tower I learned that they functioned as a society fired with genuine emotions, tempered occasionally with dull-edged reason.

Like their acceptance of washed fodder, pika behavior almost daily pointed to flexible adaptations to conditions of the moment—another paradox concerning a species reputedly chained to fixed patterns. When the gyrfalcon appeared in Green River Canyon and taloned small mammals with a speed and accuracy for which the colonists were unprepared, they doubled the number of sentinels and attempted to increase their own speed. The evolutionary force at once recorded vital experience on their memories and modified their lives in terms of that experience. They had advanced at a rate of speed that would have flabbergasted Darwin, Wallace, and Lamarck.

On the gray morning of August 8, I awoke long after daylight. Temporal misdemeanor! No reveille delegation surrounded my sleeping bag. With a small sack of granola and a dozen dried prunes, I scrambled toward Meditation Tower. Slowly the somber-faced pikas emerged from their bunkers and followed me more like goose-stepping mechanical toys than like animals facing a food shortage. Toughy, Skippy, and Rally crouched on the outer edge of the stone when I sat down. I thought it strange that they had not rushed to my lap as was their habit. Shiny and Bouncy, with unusually solemn expressions, hunkered at my feet. Smiley and Bitsy, glazy-eyed and silent, scrouged in a little closer. The colony withheld all communication. Mousey and Drummer led the four new adolescents to another boulder. Slowly Miss Humdrum and Peppy climbed noiselessly onto my lap and for the first time turned their heads away from granola. Ordinarily the "villagers" capitalized upon my intemperance when it came to indulging them, but on that morning they refused the feast.

Something had started wrong. I tried to count noses.

Crusty and Spot finally arrived with half a dozen skittish relatives from the northwest ridge, followed by the sluggard, Mopish, whom I loosely respected by then for the care he devoted to the blind Cadger. Most colonists except the new members assembled on or near the spacious Ponder Rock. Their expressions called my attention to a curdled sky, but their glassy eyes avoided direct clench with mine. Temerarius, the hermit, sat alone on his own boulder and whistled an obnoxious tune as if intentionally to disturb any deliberations that might begin among his gregarious peers. Mama Sapiens remained in her bunker. I wondered if a rainstorm might be on the way, with following frost and the end of harvest.

Still trying to ferret out some mysterious reason for their failure to awaken me, for refusal to meet me on the meadow, for turning down an offer of granola, for declining to communicate, I could only speculate on the deviatory ways of the wild. As it turned out, I squandered most of the cloudy morning on speculation.

Pondering over natural mysteries, I ransacked the landscape for anything beautiful that might possibly outlast the probable rough encounters of the day. On the talus, in camp, or along the trail, I often discovered details previously unnoticed—a new pattern of shadows, a fresh spectrum of colored lights around the peaks, the latest hit tune among the passerines, an unfamiliar sappy fragrance—and then prayed: Please, God, hold back the clock; this is paradise enough, despite the mysteries.

The sun finally broke through the clouds two full hours skyward of the Continental Divide before ten colonists consented to follow me to harvest. As yet no eye had attempted to relay a message. Not only the ewes and their lambs had moved onto the meadow but also four bull elk, their does, and six fawns. I regarded the invasion as reason enough for the pikas' refusal to come to camp. The ungulates were mowing our fodder to bare ground. In the upper Green River Lake four cow moose and their calves slopped around near shoreline, uprooted water plants, and left a brown wake of roiled sediment. Mule deer seemed to have sprouted throughout the canyon. An hour later I stoned a herd of skewbald mustangs that moseyed up the trail. Suddenly there was too much wildlife.

A partial explanation of the irritating puzzle blew up in my face.

Even while on the rock before the first trip to the meadow, I had observed Toughy, Skippy, Smiley, Bitsy, and Crusty nibbling seedpods they had cut and brought to the talus before daylight. A plant species of special significance to them, I thought, had matured its seeds during the night. A few colonists had already begun winnowing and gleaning ripe seeds for their granaries, so I was not unduly impressed—at first.

No one would have believed what I soon observed. They were shelling and eating newly ripened seeds and pods of *locoweed*, a poisonous herb notorious throughout western rangelands for its destructive effects on livestock. That was why they had failed to awaken me.

Crusty and Spot had begun to stagger and step high as if afraid of stumbling, a typical reaction to *Oxytropis*, one of several locoweed species. I picked up Crusty and turned his face away from the sun. His eyelids covered all but a sliver of his eyeballs to shade them from intense ultraviolet radiation. His pupils were rigidly dilated. For the first time, I noticed and examined a large fibroid tumor between his hind legs. Every step must have stabbed him with pain.

A gradual sickness pervaded the colony. Like domestic stock, the pikas appeared unable to resist the nocent pods—a rejection of natural truths and instinct. How little I understood those animals!

On his first visit Eagle Rock had said, "Natural law excludes human right either to question, command, or persuade."

I was to discover later that the astute pikas had reasons for ingesting the poisonous plant—justifications as valid as instincts. Still, the act shocked my unsubtle logic, because during those frenetic harvesttime days, any intermission wasted on make-believe was tantamount to insanity.

A pall of lethargy slowly enveloped the colony. Some members spent most of the day totally inactive on the shady side of Meditation Tower—an extravagance they could ill afford, even if sunny weather continued. Others left the tower and crouched in their quarters beneath the dark, maroon-black boulders.

After one harvest load I discontinued working because the intoxicated little fools had staggered after me en masse, taking absolutely no precautions against beleaguerment by emboldened carnivores poised for attack near the foot of the talus. A pine marten and a bobcat merely sprang to one side to dodge a hail of poorly hurled rocks. Alert foxes and weasels stood like sculptured bronze scrutinizing the strange course of events in Rockslideland. The predators had no doubt observed that the pika sentinels were not functioning.

With no little trepidation and other mixed emotions after that one trip to the meadow, I clung to the Ponder Rock, a one-man sentinel trying to oversee more territory than one man possibly could. I wrote a running commentary of observations in the notebook. Not until the lazy afternoon hours did the throb of life gradually return to the settlement. One young pika from a lower corridor emerged to preen his coat and scorn the meat eaters. He may have maintained a well-groomed coat during his brief tenancy in Rockslideland, but tumblebeetles found the fool's pelt, bloody and shredded, when they grubbed for scraps at the bole of the rough-legged hawk's perch.

An hour before sunset Crusty slowly floundered to the crest of the huge boulder above his and Spot's bunker, eighty feet down the talus along the northwest ridge, fifty yards below the Ponder Rock. Like a meteorite from outer space, a great gray owl arced across the scree and circled for the stoop. In the talons of that formidably fast raptor, a skunk would die before his spray reflex could function. Crusty's relatives crossed and recrossed one another's paths to confuse the advancing bird; still under the influence of locoweed, they were slow runners and slow thinkers compared with that owl. Crusty, in narcotic hypnosis, just sprawled there, ignoring high-pitched fifes of general alarm. I must have thrown a dozen rocks; but the owl swooped, side-slipped, and stooped unscathed, taloned the pika, and swished silently to the forest on the canyon parapet behind my campsite. The sandblasted scree created the impression of throbbing as it released absorbed heat.

Owing to the sudden clamor of interest, a mood of suspense swiftly vibrated across the "village." Tragically, Spot had emerged from her den at the last moment and had witnessed the kill. She called with all her strength, but must have known her mate would never return from those sickle-blade talons. I am convinced that she—and the others—knew that Crusty gave up his life because of that hideous tumor. She continued to shrill from the rock of his *felo-de-se*. Within ten minutes the same owl silenced her pitiful cries, and thus she joined her mate in their predator's metabolism.

Crusty's and Spot's refusal to take cover established beyond any doubt deliberate self-destruction in the face of painful old age. Because of emotional bewilderment, I postponed evaluation of the grotesque narcotics binge on that dreary August day.

I quote from a notebook entry written late that afternoon on the Ponder Rock:

"Frostlight had silvered the aged Crusty and Spot. Their compeers had declared a holiday from winter preparations in order to mourn in advance through the locoweed ritual . . . so it appears at this time, there being no other possible explanation. Crusty and Spot had reached inevitable destiny; but how did the rest of the colony know that August 8 would be the day of the owl? Further mourning would rob the living of time, energy, and dignity—and would do nothing for the departed; therefore, after today's respectful pause, we shall resume harvest with new determination. Maybe I'll understand later when I've had time to compare the two deaths with other suicides I have seen enacted."

Anxiety in pika expressions increased at sunset. Our parched land looked and felt as if it would burst into flames momentarily. The western sky blazed like a forest fire. My lips and knuckles had cracked from the dryness coupled with heat. Too stunned to think clearly or to accept any offered messages from my close-huddling friends, I continued to pour my feelings into my notebook, a mildly effective nepenthe when I didn't know what else to do. The colonists followed me down the talus at dusk. They milled into camp—all but Mopish, Cadger, and Temerarius. The pikas may have believed it oracular that the great gray owl, like the gyrfalcon, had come so early from arctic Canada to our forest. Crusty may have seen the big carnivore earlier. To avoid any further possibility of tragedy that day, I sent Tatters up a tree while the pikas thrashed about camp.

Owls vocalized the most pleasant night sounds— songs if you like—but owls of every clan contended with flaming hunger—incessant, insatiable, consuming hunger for the warm flesh of small mammals. The velvet softness and quiet majesty of the owls' flight, like that of giant moths within forest shadows or hillside brilliance, cloaked their silent violence that descended like a bullet from behind veils of gentleness. The impassive trees stood with apparent disregard for dramas that moved among their aisles—disregard for birds that flew about their branches or ate the fruit they dropped around their boles, disregard for whatever form of life killed or died on their duff. Shoshones, like most Amerinds, believe that owls are in dialogue with trees.

To forgo further confrontation with night birds, I used my last package of raisins to coax the restive pikas back to their bunkers. Before following me to their slope, they drank heavily from Lagomorph Creek. Most had vomited. I was unsatisfied with my conclusions regarding the locoweed. Unable to read the animal mind, I could only presume it was conceivable that pikas, like other colony animals—insects, birds, rodents and aquatic dwellers—occasionally ingest narcotics or other poisons in anticipation of death, either their own suicide or that of other colony members.

Except by chance, carnivores along the Green River watershed rarely seized alert, healthy, adult prey. They took overabundant young, aged, stupid, infirm. Easier "table." Pikas, like most colony animals, practiced birth control in order to accord with available food and housing. They accepted suicide when old age, disease, or abandonment became unbearable.

Tempest in a Doodlebug Crater

Hawks and owls swooped up and down the dusky canyon. Foxes and coyotes bounded across the talus. A bobcat climbed a tree and snarled when I pelted him. A pine marten merely moved to one side. The fact that the pikas had also seen the parade of fissipeds and dangerous birds made it easy for me to communicate that they should remain in their bunkers. I returned to camp. A feeling of distraction crept over me when I saw Tatters waiting patiently—complete with muddy feet and dripping coat—on my sleeping bag. By then he must have been more than half-grown, at least too old to stay treed until given permission to descend. I gave him what dried apricots I had hoarded and a pot of rice pudding.

The bear disclosed a serious disturbance, a good reason to be upset. I recalled seeing his loitering silhouette in the forest shadows on that tragic afternoon. He had tried to summon my attention several times, but I was too emotionally chaotic to respond. At length he drew me to a place where a boar grizzly bear had tracked the mud on *our* bank of Lagomorph Creek, a recent trail of fourteen-inch tracks. Pikas, bighorn, deer, elk, Tatters, and I would have to keep off the meadow and suspend competition for ripe huckleberries until the itinerant grizzly had browsed and moved on up the canyon; otherwise, we would face embarrassing subordination to at least 500 pounds of volcanic disposition. With two premises and a conclusion, Tatters clearly defined and simplified the problem: perception— there was no mistaking the grizzly's presence; recollection—mental images recalled that the grizzly propelled the most powerful swat in the animal kingdom; solution—the yearling attempted clarification of an unequivocal message: "Let's vacate!"

Long before sunrise next morning, a bevy of crickets fiddled file-and-scraper chords to harmonize with the softer notes of summer cicadas, all of which jubilantly suggested to me—if not to Tatters—that the grizzly bear had gone over the mountain. The insects, sensitive to vibrations, would not be sounding off if a grizzly were tramping heavily nearby. A swaying lodgepole branch directly overhead flagged my attention to the miserably uncomfortable yearling, whose pop-eyed message suggested that the impertinent grizzly had prowled about camp during the night. But Tatters's immediate meaning came through when my sleep-heavy eyes next focused upon a full encirclement of pikas standing at rigid attention around the sleeping bag. Mama Sapiens glared significantly at the yearling. Imagine the primacy in pika eyes capable of treeing a bear! An amazing accomplishment in communication. More to the point, of course, my campfire companion had received and understood my admonishment that he was *not* to besiege pikas. It was not through fear that he obeyed me. I have never seen another animal so inclined to do exactly what he thought would win my approbation.

Still chuckling before getting up, I listened to a succession of creatures that greeted dawn with funny peepings, pipings, quavers, hums, and bleats. Sunset troubadours sang lyrical and harmonious tunes for some reason or another perennially associated with dripping, poetic sentiment; but sunrise callers announced more prosaic business. The pikas didn't bat an eyelid when a skinny-shanked toad hopped through their tight formation and croaked his own matins behind their backs. Somewhere beyond the meadow, bull elk bellowed like foghorns with powerful rhythms that echoed throughout Cragrockland to announce the beginning of unusually early rut. All males involved in autumnal mating would soon respond to cryptic internal clockwork and engage in preestrual performances—a month too early. Frost seemed to ride the desert wind that morning, a more significant menace than any knight-errant grizzly bear.

The articulate pikas and I jogged directly to the meadow. I noted with disbelief that many eloquent dawn-singing birds had already migrated. Almost in the category of tragedy, bighorn rams, with sun-rimmed rumps flashing east, had nibbled to stubble every tiger lily stem. Greedy-gutty ewes had also extinguished the yellow light in remaining buttercups. Their pampered lambs had decapitated every chicory and aster blossom we had protected for the last two weeks. With calculating stares the bighorns gawked while I chopped a load of rose mallow and bluejoint stems. At length one curious old ram shuffled down to within six feet of where I was kneeling by the stream and washing fodder. The nervy sheep followed me through camp, munched granola and dried figs from my hand, then yawned. He would just as soon have yawned in the face of Gitche Manito.

To show her contempt for bighorn sheep, old Mama Sapiens, who had outtricked every agency of death for a good many years, elbowed her way through clipped goldenrods and asters to face the bellwether ram. Like a snake, the ancient matriarch waddled from the inside out. No pout ever clouded her wrinkled lips even when new ungulate urine befouled our pasture. Unable to interdict Mama Sapiens's stony gaze filled with undisguised hatred on that occasion, the shah ram finally turned and led his kind to the teasel brae above the meadow. Stares from mice have stampeded elephants.

I never heard Mama Sapiens give throat to a grievance. Her eyes generated a dazzling "smile" whenever I handed her a graham cracker tidbit or responded intelligently to one of her communications. Until I knew bears, canids, felids, and lagomorphs, I believed that man and the anthropoids were the only animal smilers. Pikas often revealed their analogous expression of mirth—always through sparkling eyes and relaxed facial muscles.

No natural force, including drought, threatened the pika food supply more seriously than bighorn sheep. Not only did they deplete and befoul meadow herbage, they also deployed over the talus and plundered one exposed haycock after the next. Sun-toasted pika garners signified a bonanza of gourmet grub to a sheep. Contemptuously ignoring my bombardment of stones, the flock transacted systematic destruction throughout the talus. I found myself uninspired to shillelagh a 300-pound ram on his native stomping ground.

The pikas used their pasture nobly and without abuse. They eked out a harvest as if counting every blade of grass, almost as if concurring not to offend the meadow by taking more than their share or damaging what they were unable to use. No pika ever defiled the flowers of annuals other than thistles. Was it possible that they respected flowers as the pledges of next year's harvest? Stems and leaves of all alpine plantlife at Square Top Mountain underwent foreshortening and stunting by altitude, drought, immature soil, and wind. Botanical species barely held their own in a fragile environment, with minimum tolerance for abuse. Apparently pikas have intuited for eons what men have only recently learned: Alpine tundra is Earth's most delicate ecological unit.

As the sheep approached brute madness in garner destruction, a tom cougar executed a lithe and silent arc that broke a lagging lamb's neck. The coordinated kill solved the pikas' problem as it had done ever since Paleozoic times. The bighorn herd clogged away and never returned that season. The lion released me from a conscience pillory, inasmuch as I had handed out goodies with one hand and tried to stone the same species with the other.

When the bighorns returned to upper palisades, the pikas went from garner to garner, probably estimating their losses. During their inspection, I sat alone on the Ponder Rock and wondered how many animals our meadow had to sustain. From notes on existing species, population estimates, predation, and a maximum of ten acres, it appeared reasonably accurate that 1,250,000 beings—mollusks, worms, arthropods, and vertebrates—interdepended upon that one pasture. For example, one bee had to eat one-fourth its weight each day in order to stay alive; this entailed visits to more than 100 plants an hour for twelve hours. Like the pikas, each meadow inhabitant *earned* a living through endless struggle.

Every time Toughy, Smiley, or Temerarius cut a thistle blossom, the act deprived dozens of bees of nectar. Fifty families of white-footed mice reproduced prodigiously in order to provide a near-starvation diet for one rough-

legged hawk family. The awesome rawness of such an antagonistic homestead imposed appalling anonymity upon single inhabitants—animals as well as plants.

Years ago I used to associate with an avid rabbit hunter, a cousin named Gray Buck, whose resistance to the truth about hard-working animals on impoverished ranges used to depress me. In proportion as experience enlightened him, however, Gray Buck altered his attitudes. Eventually he embraced the premise that a severed rabbit's foot, a Stone Age trophy with which to fortify superstitions, symbolized *bad luck* in a rabbit warren. But the most valuable lesson the young Amerind acquired demonstrated that no animal ever trusted a person with any potential to break faith; trust or distrust invariably developed through optical expression. Milton Gray Buck was the first person ever to tell me that animals communicated through their eyes.

I have often wondered how Gray Buck would have reacted to the pikas' lightning-fast system for disseminating important feelings. Speed of thought may suffer a slowdown through language, but not through the eye, because the speed of light influences that organ. As an example, Limpy hobbled at Mama Sapiens's heels most of the time. Wildlings frequently solve the problem of natural selection by allowing their weak, ill, deformed, and stupid to fall behind and into the maw of predation. Not Mama Sapiens. On several occasions I studied Limpy when his mind wandered. He rushed after a vole, played too long with a grasshopper, chased an imaginary foe. Instead of stampeding in panic after her crippled charge—or allowing him to fall victim to a carnivore—the old doe looked quickly into the eyes of the nearest pika. As if an SOS had been broadcast throughout the colony, Limpy raced to his mentor within moments after Mama Sapiens's relayed message. This performance was repeated many times.

More and more, Mama Sapiens, Toughy, and Smiley appeared to identify with my sincere concern for their welfare. Other colonists also allowed intuition to surmount instinct, probably because no living member of that colony had yet sustained a bad impression of man. My outline and odor had projected no warning image when I arrived. In their minds dwelt the profile of a benefactor with the same generic shape as their friend Eagle Rock. A volume of wisdom seemed to emanate from each pika's expression. The Great Speaker had invested amazing capabilities in *Ochotona*. Eagle Rock had invested time.

Most colony, flock, and herd animals surrender some wit for mass reproduction in the struggle to perpetuate their species. On the other hand, pikas—a colony type— live within a hostile environment that requires fullest exercise of good judgment, not numbers, to subsist. Pika adaptability obviates the need for large families in order to preserve their race.

Every trial, despair, hope, joy, and sadness of man appeared to resound in midget counterpart on the Square Top Mountain talus. Sorrow, pain, hunger, fatigue, and death horned into the experience of each pika.

With that analogy in mind during a rest stop on Meditation Tower—that August 9 morning of the sheep—I appraised the reaping so far. From every standpoint, the crop revealed glaring inadequacies. The garners—robbed by squirrels, sheep, and wind—contained less than half enough sustenance to carry the pikas through winter, even if they resorted to the heavy mound contaminated with squirrel urine.

Our hard-pressed meadow lay three-fourths denuded and now threatened with frost and continued lack of rain.

After climbing a well-anchored boulder at cliffside to explore through binoculars any possibility of cropping on adjacent barrows, instinctively I focused first on the campsite to determine whether Tatters still loitered in the vicinity. The pikas suddenly disappeared into their corridors.

There stood Marcos Eagle Rock tethering his horse to a tamarack.

Overacting to conciliation—as if I were glad to see the old rogue—I descended the slope and paced across the meadow. He smiled and extended his hand. Well—I thought—maybe the permafrost surrounding his heart had thawed a bit.

"My sister's harvest looks like that of the Little Chiefs—poor and beset with difficulties. Now we must wait a week for the combine crew. If it rains, we are ruined." He clamped an arm around my shoulders. "Are you still trying to overwhelm nature?"

"Each day I admire these little folk more—and the bear too. They have overwhelmed *me*."

"Unlike bears and pikas, man has evolved mechanically, thus losing much original perception to understand wild creatures. Fate, not man, is the Providence that hovers over Rockslideland."

Withholding comment, I waited for him to say something about floating by on a mirage—which he never mentioned. The pikas poured from the talus and milled about our feet. The Shoshone squatted and handed out rolled oats.

"I can't throw food to an animal," he said. "I would hate to have my food thrown at my feet." His visit created wild excitement among the colonists. Indulgent chomping from every jaw. Vibrant sparkling in every eye.

The shaman was doing *exactly* the thing for which he had condemned me: taming and pampering. So I told him about the granola, nuts, raisins, and hamster goodies. Instead of murdering me, he merely smiled. Something was out of character. I decided to play the waiting game.

"Men respect the Little Chiefs for what they respect in themselves—independence," he continued. He winked and smiled again.

What had reversed his attitude? Or did he plan to lull me off guard, then shoot me?

"No one can help a creature in need without helping himself," I ventured. "Catastrophe plagues these pikas day and night."

He quickly deflated that assertion. "The Earth Mother uplifts those creatures that survive her tasks."

He would never admit that his Earth Mother ever made biological boners—that she had even dealt mistake and catastrophe to one hand and success and happiness to one less worthy. As long as he continued to regard our conflict with a smile as he did on that day, I held back the speech I had prepared about his Earth Mother's lightning fires that annually incinerated millions of her babies in their cribs. Of one thing I became reasonably certain on that afternoon: Eagle Rock's relationship with the pikas was in essence no different from mine. I had violated very little of his principle.

"For years I have watched the eyes of Little Chiefs. Each of their generations has taught me also. I may have to concede that in your case as well as mine, our relationship may not be all bad. This colony has progressed remarkably in attempts to *understand man*. They may eventually become immune to the evils of taming, training, or pampering." He paused more from lack of breath than from lack of something to say.

I rushed to the fire pit, stirred the coals, threw on cones and dry twigs, fanned up a flame, and filled the coffeepot. I stoked his pipe, then mine. We sat side by side on the large armchair rock, while the pikas milled over us and clung like horseshoe nails to a lodestone.

"What did they really teach you, Marc? I'll keep it a secret if you say so."

While we drank coffee and puffed at our pipes, Drummer "eenked" out a soft, six-note song and thumped the boulder as if keeping time with her "tune." Mama Sapiens looked as if she might also be under inspiration to warble. The shaman held back an answer to my question until he was persuaded that the matron pika had changed her mind about singing. A Shoshone never interrupts man, animal, or natural force.

"They have a whistle and a song," he said, "but both come from the larynx—like a bird's call—not like the whistle we make through compressed lips. What sounds like a pika whistle is in fact a falsetto."

"Their mouths are open most of the time," I said lightly, but hoping for an observation from the learned Amerind.

"A closed mouth is a closed heart."

He listened intently to distant calls from the blind Cadger, to lengthy wails from Mopish, to short, defiant bleats from Temerarius. A few acrobatic swallows from cliffside "condominiums" perched near the campsite—for the first time. The main flock had followed mosquito and gnat swarms to lower altitude a week before. Eagle Rock spoke again, but he paused often, either to evade my question or to relish the rolling whir of a circling squadron of teal—according to him, still looking for a lead bird lost two years before. He called attention to the mournful notes of a nearby coyote whose mate a rancher had killed—five summers ago. He uttered a perfect rendition of the commonly shared vocal alarm signal of marmots, pikas, and gallinaceous birds when the gyrfalcon made a probing pass over our community. His reverence for life— his respect, affection, and empathy toward everything that stirred—represented no mere education of emotions and observations; that kind of reverence reflected a way of life. Each species issued its own proclamation in order to acknowledge the shaman's presence. I felt certain that many birds and mammals contended for his ear. From complicated facial changes and finger movements, I also sustained the distinct impression that he heard and loved in those wild voices what would probably remain lost forever to my generation.

"Never veer from an endless search for meanings," he said at last. "That was the most important thing the Little Chiefs taught me. As I got to know them better, I discovered—after ten years—that they are pluggers, lovers, and fools. Geniuses, clowns, and philosophers. And sometimes the players change roles overnight. Ordinarily consistent. Boundlessly happy creatures . . . till the weasel's or the fox's or the owl's guts begin to growl. Little Chiefs are so much creatures of habit that they have fixed times and locations for their toilet. Under constant observation, they never squat to pee but what the weasel and the fox and the owl know about it. Have you noticed? Before I knew Little

Chiefs, I *looked* with my eyes. These creatures taught me to *see* with my spirit."

I filled him in on the spree of locoweed madness that culminated in death for Crusty and Spot. I pointed to the present happiness in sixteen personalities that now darted about camp or clung to our laps. When Eagle Rock spoke, they haunched and listened as if mesmerized.

"And after yesterday's sadness, here is today's joy," he observed. "It is never a vocal hare, but a *working* hare that teaches another to work. A dying hare teaches another to die. Your Crusty and Spot taught a profound lesson. Disappointment certainly must hound their tracks, but inner wisdom grows out of it."

He paused for a few moments, combed and replaited his silver-streaked braids, then continued, knowing he had not adequately answered my question about what the pikas had taught him. "We are generally at a loss to understand most of what they try to teach us, but Little Chiefs' mental processes, like their instincts, are flawless. Curiosity leads to experiences that improve upon instinct. A coupling chain. Intelligence, energy, integrity are the links. Wisdom, judgment—even memory—last longer than steel because they improve with use."

Believing he would return to the subject, I did not press him further. He probably guessed that I would never seek to appease him.

"I've seen them scratch a lot lately with their hind legs," I said. "Galloping dandruff?"

"Yes. I saw where rodents on the meadow have taken dust baths in order to shed fleas, lice, and ticks before hibernation. One more sure sign early frost in on its way. I think it will rain shortly. The creek is at the lowest level I have ever seen it. Let's take the colony to the mouth of the canyon where they'll eat *ton-ga-ne-ba*, sometimes called *mitana*."

Eagle Rock led the way down the trail, his eyes reflecting the serene attitude of a man in harmony with the wild. He carried Peppy in one hand and Limpy in the other. I brought up the rear to prevent tagtail carnivores from picking off laggers at the end of the long procession. I carried Mama Sapiens and Toughy.

Even before we reached the rough plant, *ton-ga-ne-ba*, that I knew as Jimson weed (*Datura stramonium*), with its large white wedding-bell-shaped flowers, most pikas ran ahead to devour certain brownish, lower leaves, avoiding green parts of the plant. Within half an hour their blood-sucking parasites began to drop. Shortly before sunset they plunged into Lagomorph Creek and drowned remaining vermin as their race had probably done for centuries.

"Let's get up to the top of the talus, Bob," Eagle Rock said. "Pikas never shut their eyes on a sundown. You've also seen them open their hearts to a sunrise. They know more than the oldest trees, more than the creek that goes talking by, even more than the ancient granite. Each generation has been born with its parents' best endowments."

Fiery alpenglow beyond the bald-headed western domes brought warm renewal to the shaman and me as we sat with the pikas on Meditation Tower. I remember that quiet hour of reflection and subdued conversation with Marcos Eagle Rock as one of the happiest intervals realized in Cragrockland. He may have felt the same way, even after I told him about Tatters. He was a little provoked to learn that I had handed out treats to bighorn sheep, but he seemed to approve of everything I had done for the pikas.

"They'll hold their hush for tonight," he said at the end of amberlight. "Now what were you saying about dehydrated stew and machine-made potatoes? Let's see how you pamper a human animal that comes to your camp. I brought a carton of synthetic cream and a package of computerized pudding that I got at the Safeway."

We returned to the forest campsite. For firewood Marc broke and stacked the brittle bones of a dead aspen.

While we ate he spoke of the summer of 1955. The pikas had become infected with intestinal nematodes spread through deer manure. Fewer than half the colony members survived.

"They have lived through floods, landslides, famines, epidemics, droughts, and predation. A better lineage—prolific, strong-willed, intelligent—*because* of adversity, my friend, not in spite of it."

After the meal he carefully ashed in the campfire embers, silently fed and watered his horse, unfolded his sleeping roll near the talkative creek, threw his clothing over a lodgepole limb, and retired. He told me the altitude had brought about a breathing problem.

"Just one thought, Bob." He gasped out a series of word groups. "I see your friend Tatters. Lumbering down the trail. July has ended. Drought almost over. Storms will begin. Soon in these hills. Rain and hail. Blue wind will sing to the boreal bird . . . *Nah-Toh-Shah-Kah* [snowy owl]. Severest of all is the marsh devil. Coats the canyon with sleet. Clouds will screen the sun. Mildew will grow . . . wet haycocks. Did you see the vapor rings? Around the sunset? The garners, and therefore survival, depend upon *one* man this year. Snow's less than a moon away. September's too late. That's predictable. Beyond a doubt. Before you hit the sack, go walk for a mile or two with Tatters . . . and think! Good-night, my friend."

Although the shaman now appeared to approve of much of my work, I sensed an undercurrent of resentment that seemed to rise and fall between us—an ebbing and flowing tide that sometimes promised acceptance, sometimes threatened rejection of all I had done.

A Litany of Labor

When Marcos Eagle Rock awoke the following morning and saw my sleeping bag hedged in by haunched
pikas, he appeared more sorely distressed than angry—
perhaps both. He probably thought I had deliberately
taught them the trick.

"Whenever you tame or train Little Chiefs, they will
lose their wild," he predicted with Dantean gloom as we
finished breakfast. "You have strewn that suffering
meadow with stones—chucked at predators and grazers.
You have deprived the yearling bear of his right to grow
up as a bear. When you feed *one* bighorn, you invite disaster into the flock. They have now destroyed half the garners, half the meadow. What about the bighorn that trots
up to beg Trailmate from a bastard with a gun? Look now
at the foot of Rockslideland. Fox, weasel, marten. On the
wing—hawk, falcon, owl, eagle. Above your head in the

lodgepole—two families of owls with their eyes on the Little Chiefs. What will happen to· your friends the first time they cross this clearing when you are not here with your rocks?"

He sagged into brooding silence before we locked eyes.

"The pikas' well-being comes from full garners and full hearts," I said. "What makes a pika rejoice? Love, my friend. Love from any source he can understand. My father was also Amerind. His teaching recognized something besides lifelessness and rock in granite. What if I do rejoice the wildlife? Nothing has changed their wilderness life style."

"I'd rather be respected than loved!" he shouted as he saddled his horse. It was the first time I had ever heard him raise his voice. "What will you throw at owls when the Little Chiefs begin to harvest under the Sagamore Council [August] Moon?"

We shook hands, looked each other in the eye, still with unresolved conflict but without further hostility; yet once again he rode away unhappy that my relationship with the pikas and Tatters had become personal to what he believed an unrealistic extent. And perhaps he was right. My struggle with the aspects that I deplored in nature— her unreasoning heartlessness—externalized a sniping war with the Eagle Rock principle. He recognized it. Like the pikas, he functioned on keen-edged intuition; like his Earth Mother, he had a nasty way of kicking me out of Elysium every time I thought my foot had crossed the threshold.

Among nature's wonderful, awesome ways of truth, the emotions of mercy, sentiment, and compassion do not exist.

Regardless of viewpoint, it would be wrong to withhold any part of the account of what happened during the second half of my stay at Square Top Mountain. Immediately following Eagle Rock's sputtering departure, I swore my honor upon two resolutions: first, to work as never before, harvesting meadow, wold, marsh, and moorland until snow drove me out; second, to effect closer empathy with wildlife despite the Amerind's disapproval and his unshakable principle that all "wildlings must remain their own problem solvers."

Closer friendship with the pikas entailed ever-greater study of their daily habits, peculiarities, and "thought waves." The speed of their communicated messages still disconcerted me because combinations of vocal, optical, and body signals resulted in a fantastic amount of "vocabulary," meanings I had been unable to learn within the time frame. For example, the shifting eyeball, the flicking white-rimmed ear, and the stuttering "eenk" consistently spelled one word we all recognized: danger! But what about the steady gaze, the lifted right front foot, the silent throat, and the nod? The number of physical combinations I copied into the notebook defeated me just to think about—not to expand the combinations of purely mental possibilities. Poor communication exchange has plagued man for centuries, despite his verbal ability. It might require several lifetimes to hurdle the barriers between verbal and nonverbal species.

On a mentality plane barely below anthropoid apes, Tatters accurately picked up more optical signals than the pikas did. One stern look kept him off the meadow. Through his eyes he accepted my command to touch no pika. A single glance gave him permission to begin licking the cooking utensils. A slightly altered expression brought him instantly to my side. Through a look I invited him to wrestle. My eyes "told" him when we could hike together. In dim campfire light he received optical dismissal when I could no longer remain out of the sleeping bag. His animal neighbors had taught him a tremendous volume of optical "vocabulary." There is no doubt the bear—unencumbered by harvesttide duties and not seriously threatened by carnivores—spent more hours in "thoughtful" confrontation with my meanings than the pikas could possibly have done, notwithstanding the greater amount of time I devoted to the Little Chiefs. In proportion to body weight, a pika uses many times more brain cells than a bear and a man combined.

Tatters not only received a complicated repertory of messages but also successfully communicated a surprising variety of his own "thoughts." Once we had established body signals to accompany most optical "language," he accepted it as patently normal to ask for goodies, a hike, a harmonica concert, a scratching, a combing, or protection from his several ogres. With his eyes he imparted affection, appreciation, wit, mischief, negation, fear, bravado, and acceptance. Someone might ask, "How the hell can a bear express appreciation?" With a friendly bearpaw pat to the human shoulder, a lick across the human face, a warm nudge—and each with an accompanying optical equivalent of "Thanks!" That's how.

Something within my consciousness filled with rapture following each new "thought" engagement, whether with a colonist or with the bear—a sensation my reasoning brain still struggles to understand and perhaps will never totally accept until further research bears it out. My own projected experiment transcended classic procedures of academic thinking and traditional logic. Unfortunately, in view of the overall task, later analysis showed clearly that I failed to accomplish anything approaching the ultimate potential.

In one bona fide communication several days after Eagle Rock's departure, Toughy and Temerarius clarified their scorn for bighorn waste by leading me to plants that close-cropping sheep had uprooted, a thought suggestion I would have spurned had the plants they showed me been annuals; but they ignored annuals the sheep had uprooted. So it had to be true. Perhaps the destruction was of particular concern on account of the serious consequences they associated with continuing hot winds and low humidity. Uncanny revelations continued throughout August, the weirdest of which concerned Mopish and the blind pika. Cadger could not convey an optical message because he was blind; but vocally he demanded to share with the sluggard every goodie I brought to the boulder above his bunker. Was it instinct or appreciation for Mopish's services? Why had Cadger never feared my presence?

Whenever I placed food on Cadger's pedestal, the blind pika always murmured the same sounds, a series of pulmonary grunts released through his open, quivering mouth, calling Mopish to the feast. Mopish could have helped with the harvest and still looked after his ward, but his forces of habit were fixed. He asked the hungry to eat less so he could eat.

On each occasion after indulging Cadger, I observed Mopish because of a peculiar development. He looked me in the eye and labored to convey but one "thought," always the same "thought," slowly, as if trying to prevent misinterpretation of substance. Translated and brought to human level, his one remarkable message proposed: "We must leave this talus now and take the garners with us." I attributed the "thought" exclusively to my imagination despite his vocalizing and body movements while he led me first to the garners, then to a loose boulder. Perhaps he was referring to an early end of the meadow's productiveness. By the amount of white hair on his face I supposed him to be an elderly pika with long years of sustained observation—given that he put in no time at work, at least not during his senior pika years. As a nonverbal animal, he surveyed, appraised, and memorized situations in terms of potentials as they affected him.

*   *   *

Because of their ability to withstand shock, and because of the hereditary fortitude that braced them against trouble, the pikas derived limited pleasure even under conditions of profound seriousness. As adults with bad winters behind them, Toughy, Skippy, Shiny, Bouncy, and Mama Sapiens surprised me by occasional levity even as the meadow disappeared as a food source long before the garners would meet minimum Hunger Moon requirements. This came as a full-scale shock, because suddenly I realized that *I* bore the guilt. In pika eyes the man had become more important to them than one meadow. The significance lay in the violation of the Eagle Rock principle: The colonists now relied on me to resolve their food shortage dilemma.

Yet although the siesta on Meditation Tower had obviously become an important ritual to them, they gave up the luxury until after harvest. They accepted readily our having to make thriftiest use of every moment until the garners contained the necessary quantity of hay. They revealed no loss of well-being when we skipped that wonderful hour of rest and relaxation, but promptly generated contagious enthusiasm for the extra load of fodder we carried. To intensify my anxiety, the entire colony seemed to feel a confidence I did not share.

As August advanced, Toughy's presunrise delegation awakened me to a changing season. Melodies of water ouzel. Remote bassoon of rutting elk. V after V of southing waterfowl. Highborn bel canto of coyotes organizing into autumn hunting packs. Sibilant hisses of prowling little hobo winds decked out in scents of sage, mint, and bergamot. Morning sounds, fragrances, and movements now reflected a mood of the short-lived Wind River Range autumn. That superbly simple habit of early rising regardless of season must have added years to wildling lives.

It would be enlightening to know why distant ancestors of Toughy and Mama Sapiens never led their colonists to the affluent fields below the lakes when farmers began to shock grain sorghum and bale alfalfa. It would be gratifying to know why they chose instead to walk the narrow fringes bordering starvation and freezing. Again the Eagle Rock principle in slightly different words: Wildlings must plot their own destinies free from the notions of man.

In August we saw fireweed, goldenrod, and buckwheat seduce honey gatherers into one last decisive salvage of nectar. Varnished dragonfly wings glistened gauzier and crisper. Most butterflies and moths had taken their mid-August cues to soar on thermals over western crags when higher air density created a sensation that the mountains were bearing down upon the canyon. Deer and elk sought to establish harems in brushy hills below the lakes before September gales filled every draw with drifted snow. Crouched on the windy Ponder Rock at evening between sundown and dusk, we viewed an outback circus of wildlife retreating to lower altitude before the busy starlighter gave perspective to the sky. I often wondered why I gazed at sunsets and stars while such magnificent creatures sat on my lap. When an occasional whisky-jack decided he could improve upon the silence, an owl usually throttled the disturbance.

The pikas now harvested into the night—without my help. After half a dozen failures, I finally succeeded in holding back evening labor until we had seen the last owls, foxes, and coyotes leave for hillside hunting grounds below the lower lake. We simply sat on the rock for an extra hour of camaraderie.

Because of Eagle Rock's concern, I deplored the necessity of their nighttime work, but soon observed that almost all predation at that altitude occurred during daytime after August 10. The lack of fresh tracks on the trail indicated that most carnivorous mammals had abandoned the canyon by that date anyway. But there were exceptions, and several dangerous enemies still lurked in silent shadows—foxes, pine martens, weasels, and owls. Fortunately, no colonist disappeared during August nighttime mowing.

At night when I surrendered the little folk to their endless tasks and returned to camp, there sat the pathetically lonely Tatters, a carrion-stinky misfit in the minty fragrance of evening, waiting for the only companionship he knew, which, according to Eagle Rock's principle, would shoot him down prematurely. Too often we tend to think of half-grown bears as carefree froths of fur, brimming with Rabelaisian wit—a breed of clumsy woodland gypsies, shuffling from honeycomb to wrestling match to garbage can. But Tatters was a melancholy figure, tormented and exiled on his own heath. One local Tartarean wolverine made the bear's life miserable by chasing him up trees and out onto branches that invariably broke and painfully dumped the howling buffoon onto rocks or stickers. Four great horned dragons plagued his buttocks with vicious beak and talon slashes each time he attempted to join their quartet. When a local cougar nettled coyotes from his kill, the pack vented their embarrassment upon Tatters. If a sultan ram caught the bear foraging above juniper line, he butted and rolled the yearling downhill like a tumbleweed. A committee of longhorn elk kept him on a lodgepole branch for one full day and night because he swatted a calf out of a circle of toadstools he wanted to eat. The only time two bull moose ever cooperated for any reason was on the occasion that Tatters tried to bathe off skunk musk in the lake near their feeding shoal.

In like manner the bear also suffered several *imagined* problems, but to him they had become unassailably real: fear of thunder, wind, moving cloud shadows, falling pine cones, intimidating bumblebees, and ritualizing smaller

mammals. He was deathly afraid of snakes. His terror of nocturnal creatures compounded my headaches when he acquired the habit of storming into camp about 4:00 A.M. As if noise would bolster his sagging nerve, he stripped bark from nearby wormy deadfalls, then climbed to a branch three yards above my head where he snored like an asthmatic buffalo until the pikas arrived shortly before sunrise. The limb of his choice swayed precariously under his expanding bulk—a further example of a talent for achieving discomfort. Because he devoured every rat and mouse he could corner, I still worried for fear he might succumb to a temptation to taste pika. But he never did. As he ambled over trail, brae, and marsh, half-absorbed in the solution of his daily food problem, his only consistent tendency was to create headaches for both of us.

Concerning Tatters, I feared Eagle Rock had prophesied correctly. Had I stoned the bear the first time he appeared for a handout—had I pounded his rump with an alpenstock instead of feeding, petting, and consoling him—I would have done him a favor. He would have established independence, community peck rights, and a healthy fear of men, some of whom carried rifles with which to perpetuate paleolithic decor in the form of bearskin rugs.

On the morning of August 16 while the pikas and I shambled up the canyon to the buckwheat terraces above the distressed meadow, I watched our crisp blue sky fill with low-eaved clouds that soon clamped soggy lids over the surrounding crags. Could Eagle Rock have foreseen rain, as he had said? The terraces jutted out above the canyon as shelflike downs where the little harvesters cut stems from scattered buckwheat, saxifrage, sawgrass, and *Glyceria*. Because the heavy dark nimbus promised to put an end to the drought, I concentrated on collecting one bulky load of wind-parched fireweed stems.

Under the brewing weathermaker, bevies of cedar waxwings and song sparrows congregated on the terraces. A veritable downpour of song—a rising, swelling sound—ensued as the two species grouped into separate musters and swirled slowly down the canyon. The pikas and I exchanged glances, indicating we rejoiced to see the last of those noisy prima donnas. And then the pikas "sang!"

When falling barometric pressure called upon instinct to respond, it aroused unusual mannerisms in Toughy, Skippy, Shiny, and Bouncy—erratic movements, long jumps, shifting expressions, sparring, and frequent urination. Limpy, Rally, Gutty, Tummy, and Drummer twitched, leaped carelessly, niggled, and engaged in mild roughhousing. Drummer and Miss Humdrum "whistled" in chorus rather than singly. How quickly they recognized urgency in their elemental world of raw essentials!

It occurred to me that if uncured provender should get wet, it might mildew, ferment, and rot before sunshine could recure it following rainy weather. Even dried and sun-toasted garners required recuring in the event of lengthy soaking. Curing time in July had taken three or four days. Under August's weakening sun and unpredictable wind, hay demanded a week of clear weather to make. Their harvest, like everything else between birth and death, remained fragile and uncertain even after reaping, shocking, curing, and garnering.

We raced a panting wind in order to reach the talus to save what hay and stems the spreaders had laid out for curing. The wind won. We saw spinning funnels of half-cured stover rise from the slope like thistledown in a whirlwind. We scrambled to rescue every possible blade, stem, seedhead, and root; but most dry wisps tumbled out of reach, floated aloft on the gale, and disappeared above the perpendicular cliffhead of Square Top Mountain. Instead of rejecting any of my unwashed fireweed, the pikas now quickly divided the load, cut the stalks to size, and pulled them into dry corridors far beneath the surface.

Jumping from boulder to boulder on the shortcut to camp, I shouted and threw stones at nine adult elk who were brawling among themselves for a foothold on the path to the teasel moor—for the last green foliage in the uplands.

Spattering raindrops drew redolent spice from peppery stands of mature shepherd's-purse. The rain also directed my attention to shiny wet box elders, aspens, sumacs, and willows. On account of accelerated harvest activity, I had ignored an outburst of autumn colors—in August. But at last delicious, welcome rain showered the desiccated and starving land.

Signature of the Wind

It was easy to imagine that a wind-raveled chorus cheered from the talus when the evicted wapiti cantered down the trail toward bog and lake. Gnawed by conscience for having stoned the elk, I rushed into camp, set up a nylon pup tent, and tied a rubberized ground cloth to four trees in order to shelter my squaw wood supply and the cook pit. I felt lousy for having expelled those elk. It was possible that the pikas' vocalizing was applause for the rain, not my rock-throwing arm.

Reeking of carrion, blue mud, and wild onions, Tatters loped in, shook his dripping coat, and plopped down beside me near the stuttering campfire. It was unusual for the bear to appear that early in the day, so I walked to the trail to listen for lingering hoots from great horned owls that persisted in abusing him. Failing to locate any enemies, I returned to sit by the yearling, hoping for an inspiration that might lead to the swift invention of a deodorant. He had grown too big for me to wrestle him into the creek for a bath. His breath would have withered a buzzard, and on that particular morning he was immoderately affectionate.

A feeling of elation permeated the atmosphere as the long-delayed rain, fresh and aromatic, spattered Cragrockland. When heavy thunderbuds opened, a smell of freshness filled the canyon. On the one hand, you couldn't breathe without inhaling the fragrant atmosphere; on the other side sat the stinking Tatters.

Shivering with cold toward late afternoon, I lowered the rucksack from a bearproof limb; took out cornmeal, brown sugar, powdered milk, allspice, dehydrated applesauce, and margarine. These ingredients would simmer into a belly-warming feast of boondocks pudding. I'd show that Shoshone how cruelly I could adhere to his principle of "hands off the wildlings, man!"

Except when he shuttled his eyes back and forth and expanded his nostrils, Tatters never moved during the preparation—not even when an unusually tame porcupine, complete with entourage of two black-cowled juncos (a symbiotic alliance that frequently occurred in the Wind River Range) waddled into camp and crept under the fabric shelter to escape wind, rain, and—now—hailstones. The visitors further enhanced every circumstance of my pudding project. I planned to sit on the boulder, eat the spicy goodie in front of all of them, scrape the pot clean, and then use my alpenstock as a cudgel to drive the animals into the rain and down the trail. Oh, yeah! Good for toughening them, according to Marcos Eagle Rock; that should make his ailing heart sit up and pump for joy. His eyes would sparkle approval. He would never know that my real, underlying motive was to celebrate the arrival of rain.

While a woodpecker tattooed a pagan drum song on a

dead and barkless lodgepole shell, I allowed the tasty food
to cool and spread its sugary spiciness up and down the
squally canyon. It must have been the heady air, for suddenly I regarded Eagle Rock as an ambivalent, hypocriti-
cal, jealous old man.

The drenched porcupine and his junco buddies ignored me and the bear while they slurped their allotment
from the same aluminum plate; Tatters, oblivious to all the
world except his own sweet, gooey serving, took care of
the pot. I ate from a cup. The project was a total success.
My conscience and I rocked back and forth on the armchair boulder and laughed until we cried. The juncos led
the porcupine to a new stand of lodgepole seedlings. The
pudding merely whetted Tatters's appetitite, so he rushed
into the storm to search for something more solid.

As a man who had spent a lifetime among wildlings in
the Green River region, Jim Bridger declared that the
"Wind River Mountains were created by God to hide the
devil in . . . no fit place for 'possums, prairie dogs, and pal-
frey-poachers." I had begun to think of the range as big
enough to support everything from the smiles of tender
pikas to the frowns of rampaging grizzlies.

By dark the rain and hail still snare-drummed against
the tarp, but an occasional breakthrough of the sterile
sliver of a new moon presaged favorable weather for the
next few days' harvest. We might expect none of the pow-
dering heat of July, but the clean scent of chinook air now
permeated the range.

To my practical side, the approach of rain, inevitable
wind, and early frost foretold misery and starvation. The
pikas had garnered little more than half their winter requirement. They sang and skittered about the talus as always when rain pelted them, but they shrieked and
grumbled when hailstones forced them into their bunkers.
Nevertheless, among the last sounds of day, that first
windy squall whispered a subtle warning, an admonition

more sensed than heard—Eagle Rock's reminder of what lay ahead in September.

About 2:00 A.M. I whistled an answer to Skippy and Bouncy, who called from the talus. Their screech was not the usual cry of alarm, but I dressed as quickly as possible, grabbed the flashlight, and climbed the wet granite in bone-chilling wind to determine what had caused the extraordinary cry. The chanting pikas had just returned from the meadow with their last load of fodder for the night. Many of the colonists had not stopped working just because of a little rain. Although darkness prevented my seeing the eyes of Mama Sapiens and Toughy, when they poked their noses into my cupped hands, I sensed that all was well; so I slogged back to the tent and shivered to sleep with patched-up peace of mind. Skippy's and Bouncy's new cry became the regular quitting-time whistle at night.

At daybreak the little lagomorphs scrambled through camp and shrilled their disbelief. Their "eenks" flooded the canyon as if they were trying to wake up the dawn. The granola man had lost his mind. They had never seen a tent.

Sunrise revealed water-stained patterns on the swarthy cliff bulkhead behind Rockslideland. Wet blotches 1,700 feet long reminded me that the talus had to distribute and absorb the full volume of whatever runoff poured from Square Top Mountain, because the top of the mesa tilted slightly toward the talus! At that instant those artistic water stains indicated damage to pika garners.

After leading me to devastation far worse than I had anticipated, the pikas sat for no more than ten minutes surveying their losses. Much of the wet fodder appeared irredeemable. All the surface garners required recuring, reweaving. When we had spread the sloppy provender to dry, eight colonists and I climbed down to the depleted meadow. Even after a soaking rain, the remaining few blades of grass and twisted shepherd's-purse lay flat on the ground, too long without moisture for revival. Under pretext of sentry duty or salvage, most of the pikas refused to follow me to the meadow. They knew before I did that the pasture had produced its last load for the season.

From the shiny wet gables along the divide to the range's granite foundations, the Wind Rivers bore the clean signature of sunshine and wind. At this juncture sun and wind could ransom a jeopardized harvest, but all the pikas scolded the greedy gusts for having developed such an appetite for their fodder. I watched one voracious current after another rake up and snatch away our hard-earned loads of curing hay. The Red Desert wind had robbed us of our meadow; the norther now stole our garners.

So we began again, as we had done in the wake of squirrels, bighorns, drought, and whirlwinds. Older colonists probably knew that rain, coming tragically late as it did shortly before Indian summer, predicated ruin to fodder. Consequently, they joined the spreaders and worked as if effort alone would save their winter pantry. Hence, those of us in search of fresh stems on the higher canyon shelves pushed ourselves even more relentlessly. Hour by hour, load by load, I saw in their eyes that adversity symbolized no great catastrophe, nothing more than one raveled hem of everyday life on the barren slope. Older bucks voiced what I interpreted as complaints whenever misfortune buffeted them, but their does resumed work as if nothing had happened. To be sure, ceaseless labor shaped dull attitudes, but in principle, the Great Hand had designed a deeper mesh for pika character, a confirmation of the old shaman's rule: "They must remain their own problem solvers." By sunset the amount of recovered and restacked fodder bolstered the shaman's thesis.

Although leadership may have figured as an unnecessary commodity—even when the colony stood to lose essential winter supplies—Mama Sapiens, Toughy, Skippy, Bouncy, Smiley, and Rally proved themselves of greater value than others to the total community. On the other hand, Mousey, Scotty, Pliny, and to some extent Miss Humdrum at times may have performed below colony criteria. It was the mother pikas that embodied the real vertebrae of the "village" spine, especially during recuring and regarnering. I suppose you could argue that a prototype of leadership blossomed when the mothers put their offspring to work on those wet haycocks.

When Square Top's crags echoed the voices of other species, Skippy, Bouncy, and Bitsy exhorted the young to listen selectively. Some of those sounds voiced the difference between life and death. When it appeared to me that Mama Sapiens took too much time to instruct her charges, I decided she was probably teaching an exercise in concentration. Even the newcomers sat patiently and watched the older does drill dexterity into the awkward limbs of their offspring.

Within most youngsters the potentials of pikadom begged for development. They were eager learners. Some observers might argue that extra training merely gilded the lily of instinct and that young pikas would have acquired their knowledge without "formal schooling." It was significant that on the talus, as elsewhere, sophisticated parental coaching coincided with small families. Only the rarest occasional shirker sullied a mother's record, like the young dandy who preened himself in defiance of the raptor. Schooling was not without merit.

Youthful pikas created many humorous scenes on the slope as on the meadow—crudely woven garners that fell apart in the slightest breeze, awkward courting by young machos, clumsy dealings with bees, wasps, and hornets. I never laughed *at* any pika. I often laughed *with* them. Like other wild animals I have known, they reacted as if keenly attuned to the difference. Only when the rough-legged hawk's flight turned out more spectacular in daring than in accurate stoop—when he lost a cloud of feathers in an attempt to dive between two boulders—did we all laugh at his flamboyance. When a water snake choked on a frog too big to swallow—and the frog hopped away singing—we sat and laughed at the serpent's cupidity.

Older pikas had a funny bone more difficult to tickle, but nearly every day they found some reason for a ready "smile." With amazing regularity, Smiley looked into my eyes and "smiled" when Temerarius sidestepped one of Drummer's intentional encounters. Smiley "laughed" at his mate, Bitsy, when she tried to lift more than she could carry. Toughy and Skippy "smiled" when I shook a finger at Gutty and Tummy for overeating. All evidence of "laughter" radiated from their eyes, never from lips or vocal cords. I cannot recall having seen a pika heckle or tease another in order to create a seemingly funny situation, although at times even the most serious engaged in scrimmages that appeared to accomplish pure nonsense. But no universal key to the pika sense of humor ever turned up.

Except for an occasional upbraiding of the sluggard, Mopish, there was never a consistent example of a quarrelsome nature. To my knowledge no fight ever broke out that summer between two Square Top talus pikas; for colony animals living in close proximity, it was indeed rare that minor arguments occurred.

Because they had moiled through half the rainy night in order to make up losses as well as to meet seasonal quotas, I coaxed the weary colonists to the Ponder Rock for a siesta on the afternoon following the storm. Toughy, Skippy, and Rally fell asleep on my lap. Shiny, Bouncy, Smiley, Bitsy, and Mousey napped near my feet. Temerarius stretched out full length on a boulder near his private cliff. Cadger and Mopish dozed on a big rock below us, while twelve of our fellow workers—mothers and their young, sentinels, decoys, and Mama Sapiens—sprawled about the sun-drenched boulders between the rock and the meadow. A few slept in their bunkers. Because they had worked night and day, I showed my willingness to do guard duty so that the colony might catch up on much needed rest.

Sometime during that siesta on Wednesday, August 19, I fell asleep along with the drowsy pikas. A single shriek awakened us all. While we slept, a marten and a rough-legged hawk timed their strikes to coincide. Two pikas lost their lives. For a moment I imagined Eagle Rock running down the trail, snickering and shaking an accusing finger. What he had said about my softening the pikas rang in my ears. How insensitive I had grown to the bastinadoes of that stone-knuckled environment! Somehow I had deceived myself into believing that "hands off, man!" didn't apply to me. Regaining approbation of conscience entailed a lengthy battle.

The tragedy confirmed earlier observations that carnivores methodically studied and selected prospective victims sometimes for days ahead of killing time—a sleepy old male, a slow-witted female, a careless young sentinel, a cripple, a nonconformist. As resourcefully intelligent creatures, hunters did what had to be done, and the pika race benefited—according to a book I had read.

Then the strangest thing happened on that lamentable afternoon. Apparently the elders knew an enemy would strike again shortly. I watched in amazement as an emboldened weasel climbed the talus. With a display of hatred and violence I thought impossible for pikas, eight bucks and Mama Sapiens formed a vigilante committee. At an amazingly preplanned moment, they met and surrounded the weasel. Carnivores don't always succeed.

The colonists probably knew their own foibles as well as strengths, but wisely concealed both from outsiders. On this occasion they broke with tradition, saw and conquered through personal courage—not through escape—an intolerable community threat. Courage came from hearts, regardless of deficiencies, not from size, number, custom, or wit. Danger provided the crucible for testing true courage. Square Top Mountain pikas were never as small as their size.

After placing the weasel's shredded body on a table-top boulder near the meadow for a cleanup crew of ravens, I may have agonized more than the pikas while we watched. Now that I had let them down—now that compromise had forced them to kill—I wondered whether sunshine and trust would again enhance the harvest work that remained.

Temporarily exempted from death by dispatching a half-starved weasel, twelve colony members returned with me to the buckwheat terrace for our next load of herbage; others resumed the urgent business of spreading and turning green and wet fodder for proper drying. Garnering now became more of a family affair. Rockslideland had emerged a corporate body. While silent sadness lingered throughout the village that afternoon, a new dimension of independence shone in pika eyes, unaccompanied by a single cocky exhibition of the win syndrome that invariably inflates conquering baboons, mules, and razorback hogs.

Incredibly out of character for the season, one invasion after another of large and small grazers from lower altitudes overran and quickly annihilated what remained of easily reached provender. After the brief rain, a thermal updraft of Indian summer encouraged a hostile incursion of mustang horses, deer, elk, coyotes, and bobcats whose greens or prey had mummified under continuing drought in the Green River Valley.

Voice of the Mirage

Neither brooders nor dealers in sentiment, the pikas quickly rekeyed their lives to the immediate milieu of harvest. Elders appeared to remember the dead. Although they sat for periods of reflection after a death, they contended more with the compelling forces of *now*: weather, hunger, competition, and security.

On the day after the first aggressor's death, a second weasel arrived with a vigorous nose for warm blood. After appraising the surroundings, however, he decided against establishing residence on the talus: stares of perching owls and hawks revealed fervent craving for weasel flesh. He also observed that raptors kept the slope under constant surveillance—that two or three sharp whistles from pikas brought a hail of rocks each of which weighed more than he did. To offset the insidious, the crafty hunter took up canyon lodging under a safe boulder halfway between the marsh and the talus. He became successful in colonies of mice and wood rats.

Despite weather and predation adversities, the pikas and I persisted in cropping; but each time we descended the talus and headed toward the terraces, I saw distant looks instead of sparkling enthusiasm in the eyes of Toughy, Shiny, Smiley, and Mama Sapiens. Time and fodder were running out. They may have questioned by now my ability to lead them to ample reaping. Without man's reinforcement, it is doubtful that normal pikas would have pursued food supplies farther than fifty yards from their bunkers. They would have starved.

Of late an owl in a hollow tamarack down the canyon had called repeatedly without an answer. Adult does may have regarded the incessant outcry as sufficient reason for communicating anxiety and unrest to younger animals. Shoshones regarded the phenomenon as an omen of death. An overall nervousness prevailed. The pikas stayed very close to my heels when we traveled for fodder. August became a time of side-glanced apprehension. Limpy and Peppy seldom strayed from Mama Sapiens's shadow. Before that time all pikas had preferred nearby sedges and grasses to forbs, but now they gulped any remaining vegetation rather than wander from troop safety in search of favorites. Cadger clung within whispering distance of Mopish day and night. Temerarius, by contrast, stood pat on his prerogative to give up neither solitude nor temerity.

Neither August's hard times nor the vast differences between me and the pikas prevented measurable expansion of understanding. Mama Sapiens, the interpreter, came more often to my rescue when impasses developed. An example of her intercession occurred on the afternoon of August 22.

Lying on my belly on closely cropped grass, I faced the twelve colonists with whom I enjoyed most fluent empathy. No fodder remained on the buckwheat wold. The pikas sat as if waiting for me to lead them to another source. In order to distract troubled minds, I attempted for the hundredth time to communicate the sincere fondness I bore in my heart for them. With obvious effort on their part, these friendliest twelve tried hardest to understand me, but never before that afternoon had they quite comprehended more than an outer fringe of the affection I felt toward them. I had accomplished profound personal changes and adjustments in order to receive fewer than a score of their messages. Only through reduction and simplification had I been able to broadcast several of my own rudimentary feelings—but as yet, not love.

When Mama Sapiens brought Limpy to me on the twenty-second, little doubt remained in my mind that the colony had engaged in some form of "dialogue" concerning their Gulliver. Extremely inhibited and timid, Limpy would not have approached me with his problem: a front paw continuously infected because of an embedded thorn.

With all animals time is *now*. Readiness for acceptance rarely tolerates procrastination. I rushed to camp for tweezers and iodine. After lengthy vocal and optical exchanges with Mama Sapiens, the whimpering, cringing Limpy allowed me to take his forearm between my thumb and forefinger. While other colonists stared in bug-eyed silence, I squeezed Limpy's pastern until the paw became numb and blanched, at which time I turned it over carefully, removed the thorn instantly, and applied disinfectant. He relaxed completely during the ordeal, but not until I released him did he take his soft-brown eyes from my face. From that day on, Limpy regarded me as his closest friend next to Mama Sapiens.

Thus the colony acquired specific insight into human affection through physical performance as well as by way of optical assurances.

*   *   *

Until Limpy's foot improved, I carried him when we resorted to the marsh for fodder. Distance and trailside hazards bedeviled us. I hated the harrowing experience of Pied Pipering the colony as a troop along a trail beset for 300 yards with carnivores whose food supply had also dwindled to its lowest annual ebb. I shuddered when laggers tried to follow as an afterthought.

On the morning of the twenty-third we sat trying to regain breath on Meditation Tower after one round trip to the marsh and back to Rockslideland. I had delivered a heavy load of high-calorie willow shoots that required no sun curing. A gusty breeze invaded the canyon. Weather moods best epitomized wilderness freedom, especially in the adventurous temperament of the wind: high-spirited, wild, nonpredaceous. With up-cupped ears, squinty eyes, and dilated nostrils, Toughy, Temerarius, Shiny, and Mama Sapiens tested each gust for a weather vagary before we undertook our next trip. The pikas always looked forward to a lusty blow, although they may have learned the full disastrous truth of the winds of drought.

Meteorologists claim that animals have no way of predicting weather; meteorologists hold an even worse record.

Anticipating a change through sensitivity to barometric pressure (pikas have other built-in seasonal mechanisms, so why not a barometer?), the colonists refused to return to the bog for the rest of that day. By the time I struggled up the slope with my next load, they had lugged all uncured fodder into the labyrinths. A dozen familiar characters sat on the Ponder Rock, balancing in the sun and wind, devoting resolute attention to cleaning toenails. Like bathing, daily manicuring illustrated a very social community project—and what better occasion than just before a storm?

By then each pika had become wondrously important to me. Upon discovery of distinguishing differences

among the younger animals, I assigned names in my anec-
dotal records as I had done earlier with adults. Extensive
observable changes appeared in every youngster, especially in attitudes toward me. As they not only accepted
my presence but also became friendly and trusting, I failed
utterly to restrain human susceptibility toward personal
attachment. The Eagle Rock principle, I admit, never ex-
cluded human love for wildlings; it categorically prohib-
ited man's meddling in their intrinsic affairs. A month
earlier I would hardly have believed it possible that a multitude of cottontaillike creatures could have captivated
human attention so extensively; but having struggled to
communicate with them in a limited way and having
worked hard to follow intelligently many of their behav-
ioral patterns, I had been projected irretrievably into every
aspect of their lives. I worked for them now as if each hour
were my last on Earth.

Day by day I had studied and conceded Cadger's declining will to carry on. I brought him fresh clover and rose
mallow seeds when I could find them, roasted nuts and
sugared cereal as long as my supply held out; but his song
and whistle went sour and soon they were heard no more.
Possibly realizing that his afflictions were permanent and
worsening, he may have recognized that blind, arthritic old
age prevented any reconciliation with his community. He
began to expose himself recklessly. Ethologists say that
man alone knows he must die and dwells on the subject;
yet, in my own mind, I am convinced that Cadger also
contemplated death, even if scientists can prove otherwise.

During a rest stop on the afternoon of the twenty-
third, twelve colonists and I sat daydreaming on the Ponder Rock when a sentinel sirened an alarm announcing the
weasel.

"This way, Cadger!" I shouted and kept talking in
order to guide him toward the tower while I stepped over
to the "ammunition dump," a pile of baseball-sized rocks

amassed to reinforce eviction notices to unwelcome so-
journers. But instead of feeling his way toward safety as he
usually did, he ran beneath a boulder to the corridor that
led into his subterranean retreat. Unhurried, the weasel
followed.

Healthy animals with sight could easily and quickly
outmaneuver a weasel on the rocks; but if a pika panicked
and rushed to a bunker, he would find himself without
prospect of escape. Invariably the narrow corridors ended
in cul-de-sac chambers. The weasel, smaller in diameter
than a pika, could rush in and corner his victim. Until my
arrival, Cadger had escaped predation by following Mopish's subvocal signals to safety when an enemy prowled.

The colony sat spellbound and stared from one to another. As an aged pika, Cadger neither cried for help nor
moaned from pain during his killer's embrace in that dark
grotto. When he felt his throat tighten, he probably sputtered a final stammer as if conveying a message of reassur-
ance to the weasel. On the Ponder Rock, Mama Sapiens
gathered half a dozen youngsters about her. Through im-
perious stares and low mutterings, she may have revealed
a mystery of life. Sunny and Teeny issued the sounds of
grief.

After draining his victim's blood and eating the liver,
the weasel consummated his responsibility to the ecosystem by dragging Cadger's body to the surface and placing
it on a boulder for fox, raccoon, or raven. To avoid competition, ravens picked up bloodless carcasses and carried
them to the "table" above the cliff—above the north face
where the Earth Mother had carved a profile that in sundown light bore a striking resemblance to Marcos Eagle
Rock.

The death scene was always cleaner when carnivores
other than weasels seized a pika, because the colony never
saw the dead body again.

Contemplating that prostrate form on the rock where

the red-mouthed hunter had left it, I recalled how Cadger often outwhistled the wind through his funny little clown-like mouth. I called him the whistlebard of Rockslideland, but there had been no channel through which to convey the compliment.

Mopish ran to the rock, haunched, looked me in the eye, and shrilled for five minutes, clearly an abusive denunciation. The wind joined in the diatribe.

Although Cadger's killing enacted predation more ancient than Mesozoic ancestors of all present-day species, older still was the wind. Everything on Earth has changed except the wind. The same gale that kneaded primordial ooze, that bore away the final effluvium of the last dead dinosaur, that fanned hot Hannibal's brow, now fingered through each pika's whiskers. Unchanged in any way. Wind that nodded anemones and poppies taught man and pika to whistle. That same eternal, immutable personality shoulders mile-high thunderheads, five-mile-high aircraft, ten-mile-high radioactives that man sacks from the tombs of the Desert Makers. Wind has figured in every surface change since Earth became a solar satellite. Yet wind has never allowed itself the slightest change other than velocity.

It was the Red Desert's voracious gale that suddenly mesmerized the canyon. Heeding the onslaught of a dusty tornado with distrust, I ran from the talus when steady, counterclockwise gusts began to rise, twist, and orchestrate across the sprawling wilderness like octaves from Beethoven distorted through amplification. The lakes tossed and writhed in their troughs, tossed frothy spume onto their sandy shores. The vindictive gale-force wind gulped our fodder as if to prove that no species had a right to hoard anything in a land of no possessions. Each blast hissed toward the west flank of the cordillera and piled yeasty clouds against the spires, minarets, and buttresses along the divide. A giant horde of invisible weasels tore at Mount Sacajawea's jugular veins, spewed dusty-red banners during the violent embrace.

Jumping from boulder to boulder on the way back to camp, I paused long enough to stone a swaybacked bull moose from the meadow. I looked up at the pikas. They clung to narrow crests, facing away from the tempest that raveled their calls and sandblasted the naked boulders beneath them. For intensified sensation, they always wanted the wind to blow their fur against the grain. The colony may have known that I too participated in the swelling storm's frenzy. We shared a peculiar elation that only wind could arouse. Although savage twisters held up harvest and further impoverished pika pantries, we still indulged ourselves in every droning mistral for the sheer vagary it afforded. While I sat in the shuddery wood, listening to the churning Lagmorph Creek and wondering where Tatters had holed up, whirlwinds swept down and broomed away with sandpapery rasp every loose leaf of alder, willow, and aspen. The grating discord lisped like a stuttering ghost groping for a foothold. Tempestuous spirits caused dust particles to swirl in the slanting forest sunshafts, caused them to throb and flicker with spooky personalities like the wraiths of Shoshone legend.

Overhead, scattered cumuli smeared the dusty peaks for an hour; then the whole sky looked as if it were drawn by cloud teams. Though the wind howled in their ears, sanded their eyeballs, and distorted their voices, the pikas sang anyway, savoring that boisterous aspect of autumn.

A steady sundowner gale at length swished away most of the clouds and swept the untidy sky clean of the Red Desert dust that had draped the Wind River Range with haze. Because of the rising, swirling particles in the air, the moon yielded more light for witchcraft in the early evening shadows. The blast gave ponderous grace to nighttime movement. According to Eagle Rock, the wind, like the trees, had a distinctly notional personality at night. Ancient tamaracks voiced organlike tones as if to outperform the sharp-tongued westerly. During the daylight hours the wind blew, but at night it howled and shrieked savage murder.

Because of fire hazard while the storm raged, and because Tatters had found refuge too distant for an evening visit, I ate a cold supper and crawled into the down bag. As always of a restless night, I regarded my comfortable tent and mummy bag as sensual excesses in scrimpy Cragrockland. The tent fly sheet popped like clusters of Chinese firecrackers. At midnight several pikas shouted distress signals between lispy gasps of the gale. I crawled from the tent, dressed, and headed for the talus.

That was the moment I challenged my presence in Cragrockland. I shouted that Eagle Rock had profaned his own dogma by inviting me to help with the harvest in the first place. On that blustery night nothing really made sense. The gale had wormed ghostly fingers under many subsurface garners, scooped them out, and scattered well-cured provender across the talus and far beyond.

Toward 3:00 A.M. the breathy, saw-toothed roar broke up into spasms of lesser intensity. By flashlight the pikas and I vaulted about the talus, plunging with headlong drive to recover what stems we could find. Orion's belt had slouched over the western crestline by the time I fell back into the tent. Our accomplishment was hardly worth the candle.

Dawn had almost reddened into sunrise before the pikas stole to the tent. Toughy peered through the mosquito netting. From the expression in his eyes I assumed that the windstorm had blown itself out. For that information I handed him a cashew nut. Trembling cloud towers and drawn-out mares' tails presaged favorable curing weather—provided we could find anything to cure.

The yellow rays of sunrise revealed neither bewilderment nor defeat in the colony. In all probability no pika had closed his or her eyes during the big blow. But no amount of loss precluded one moment's enjoyment of the squall. They were born in Wyoming's wild gales, lived and died in them. Now they restlessly awaited the day's work and recovery of as much scattered hay as possible. The morning air came in lusty puffs, between which long skeins of teal rose from the lakes, soared into the flyways, and avoided the Continental Divide through southern passes.

By noon only a hint of a breeze loitered in the canyon, like the deceptively soft auditory illusions that sometimes accompanied Wind River Range mirages. Garners that younger pikas had constructed too near the surface had suffered extensive damage, and we recovered no more than a short bushel from what the corsair wind had strewn. Consequently, we faced a loss that had to be made up—a month too late.

No amount of poverty or environmental hardships disposed any pika toward theft from another's pantry. *Ochotona* never accumulated wealth at a neighbor's expense. In truth, they had erected most garners along contiguous corridor runways, the complex I called Main Street, where for ages entire populations had converged to eat during winter Hunger Moons. Among all wild animals, honor distinguishes their relationships with their kin— more so than strength, cunning, and compromise.

In the windstorm's wake many starving carnivores, themselves victims of the all-summer drought, ventured up the watershed of the Green: a slovenly coyote that slunk with his tail tucked tightly between his legs (in itself a sign of indigence), a slouchy-paunched bobcat, a scrawny skulk of foxes, several windblown eagles whose companionship with clouds had suffered, and a hunger-crazed array of whopping big owls.

Song of the Night Bird

The unculled and famished horde of invaders ducked about with a healthy fear of man. They fled from meadow and talus under a barrage of stones; but the resident fissipeds, now arrogant and defiant, lurked barely out of rockfire range. Even their reduced number constituted a more dangerous threat than the desperately starving newcomers, because they had memorized our defenses, knew every habit of man and pika on the talus.

After the windstorm my friends and I worked on far-flung and niggardly pastures to replenish the storm-razed garners. Colonists ate on the spot several gourmet delights: late alpine clover and second-growth saxifrage; but the summer brilliance and streamside abundance had disappeared. We cut tender willow and aspen shoots, ripe buckwheat clusters, alpine shintangle—any vegetation that would tide the settlement over until the following June's Moon of the Moose Child. Lacking a vital kernel of substance, plants whose flowers had spent themselves on summer wind without setting seedpods provided the poorest fodder come winter. At first we rejected those. At no time now did any pika discard herbage from my packrack loads, provided I washed it in the creek before delivery.

Light frost on the night of August 25 rendered the marsh almost useless as a food source for the rest of that year. Marshland feeders—rodents as well as hoofed animals—moved to compete on the upland downs. Bobcats, raccoons, foxes, and coyotes at that time became grazers, a normal restyling of diet among carnivores other than the weasel clan.

Even though the pikas themselves had first predicted to Eagle Rock the probability of early winter, they frequently deviated from character by playing the prodigal for hours during those last days of Indian summer when I thought they should be working. Temerarius, whose garners had suffered neither loss nor deficiency, romped and played with Peppy, Rally, and Tummy, whose cupboards would be empty by January. Mousey and Scotty crouched for hours and stared blankly into space. Drummer, Miss Humdrum, and Gutty squandered precious time in lengthy songfests with the four exogamous exchange youngsters. Mama Sapiens, Toughy, Shiny, and Limpy continued to bring in fodder. In light of their forethoughts of a short season, most adult males now fussed and scolded unless I rushed up and down the slope without rest stops or hiked far afield in search of new crevices and shelves to glean. Even with occasional excesses and suspension of obligation, no human being could have followed the industrious little beasts on every round trip they

made day and night. In times of seriousness they outper-
formed the most intensely sobersided animals I have ever
known.

What I called autumn at Square Top Mountain was
much shorter than the season we know at lower elevations.
Nevertheless, that short-lived interval between August 10
and September 10 amounted to a changing period with
tantalizing character and startling vividness. Hardwood
leaves in three days waxed as brilliant as any summer
flower. The air grew crisp, redolent, and delicious to
breathe. The little man with the crystal brush quickly
coated youthful greens with tawny yellows and burnished
reds. Exposed profiles sparkled with outlines of early
morning rime; but the woods still emitted the ferment and
pungence associated with spring. And although the last alpine sunflowers that bordered timberline had faded, their
seed would flower again after winter sleep. Autumn leaves
fell—not as skin, teeth, and hair, but as a purge to bring renewal that forever perpetuates youth in perennials. Night's
vaultlike chill provided an impetus for pikas to sleep
closer together, to emit warmth and promise of winter
mating and spring babies.

With the end of drought, fall's brief interlude exalted
fruitfulness, a short period when canyon dwellers lifted a
mirror and said, "This we have accomplished. Now it is
time for dreams." The season suggested that death itself
cocooned but an uneventful chrysalis awaiting future
rebirth.

Our foreshortened autumn brought about a remarkable series of adaptations. Herbaceous plants no longer
available, the pikas instinctively knew to dig and clean tu-
berlike roots of sweet cicely, dock, chickweed, and horse-
radish. When fodder fell before the scythe of frost,
marmots, chipmunks, and chickarees bypassed shortages
as well as the rigors of five Hunger Moons by hibernating
on hoarded fat, which may have accounted for the social

cleavage between lagomorphs and rodents. Granivorous birds and grazing mammals, unable to cope with the radical adjustments necessary for high-country survival, hit the trail for the Green River Valley where the guns of "sportsmen" awaited them.

Serpents hibernated when young mammals grew too large for easy swallowing. Very few reptiles stored extra weight. Who ever saw a *fat* snake? Marten, mink, weasel, and skunk became locally scarce when they themselves fell prey to gyrfalcons, owls, and departing foxes and coyotes.

After the latest windstorm, a detail of six adult pikas followed me to a sun-flooded shelf fifty yards above the buckwheat flats. The area entailed more downright labor for one short packload than any so far. We returned to the talus with buffalo grass, grama, and red ray that had already hayed and toasted on the canyonside's steepest exposure. With a full load, I staggered back down the route, reflecting absentmindedly upon the seeds we scattered from the dangling ripe spikes as we plodded along.

Rising unexpectedly from the talus, a red-tailed hawk flapped furiously, crossed the canyon, and disappeared in the forest. The large raptor carried prey; but on account of the sun's position, I could only guess what the bird had taloned. The pikas, huddling close to my feet, silently watched the hawk's flight with such intense scrutiny that I interpreted their squinting to be the result of knowledge I did not have. Their mood changed on the spot.

Unable to locate Drummer among the harvest workers, I rushed to the nearby boulder under which she lived. She was not there. The happy little spinster, who always drummed approvals and disapprovals with her hind paws, shared a corridor with Rally. Mama Sapiens and Toughy sniffed a fresh blood stain on a rock near where we had left her to help rearrange wind-damaged garners. With the candid grace of simple folk, Shiny, Mousey, and Rally lingered at the bunker entrance and communicated to my eyes a message I didn't need.

To hawk, owl, fox, and weasel the colony paid tithe, a symbolic price tag on what the poet called the "toll" of life. Tithe balanced the population equation. Master link in the food chain.

Notwithstanding losses, the adversities the colony had suffered never proved calamitous to the species. Eagle Rock had recalled the summer of 1955 when his Little Chiefs ignored contamination in the form of intestinal nematodes in deer manure on the meadow. The parasite had all but wiped out the Green River colonies; yet their species survived. In times past, flood, avalanche, earthquake, landslide, forest fire, and predation—one crowding the heels of the next—had failed to annihilate. In the long run a prolific lineage, strong-willed, healthy, and intelligent, survived even cataclysmic misfortune—according to the Shoshone.

Mopish, the sluggard, and Temerarius, the hermit, somehow held out as living exceptions to pika code. Mopish underwent no change whatever following Cadger's death. He took over the stores that Crusty and Spot had garnered. A choosy wastrel, he ignored cast-off fodder, never once descended the talus to work with the rest of us, never stood sentry duty to my knowledge—a mutation or divergence from the working-class pikas. When he ate from Main Street garners, his peers uttered meaty invective, if I read the "language" correctly. Yet they tolerated him.

Without the responsibility of caring for Cadger, Mopish dashed about impatiently waiting for me to take rest breaks on Meditation Tower. I may have been the only creature in Rockslideland to lend him an ear. On the talus he followed me like a whining puppy; and although we locked eyes frequently, my reception at first was too prejudiced ever to assimilate more than a fraction of the old charlatan's message, which, in effect, suggested over and over that the colony should move to less shaky surroundings. His eyes often directed mine to another talus farther up the canyon. He panicked and shrieked whenever big rocks moved slightly in normal scree settling. On five specific occasions I allowed him to lead me to loose boulders I could rock back and forth. Elder pikas sat stolidly around the tower and deliberately looked in another direction while Mopish attempted—but failed—to convince me. Perhaps they didn't despise him as much as I thought they did, but they spurned and ignored him. He went down in my notebook as a hysterical old man. Somehow he charmed the exogamous exchange youngsters.

Temerarius basked in his hermitage. He represented a paragon of pika probity, amassed his own larder, contributed some to the Main Street garners, snubbed me with malice aforethought, and except during occasional sentry duty or wild fandango with young females, fraternized with few adult pikas. Naturally, he and Mopish were not on "speaking" terms. When the colony sang, he whistled a different "tune." That the community put up with a hermit and a parasite remained among the several unsolved mysteries of the hamlet.

Further enigma—with artful complications—surrounded a decoy system that went into effect whenever sentinels whistled an alarm. At Mousey's signal, Mama Sapiens, Limpy, Peppy, Rally, and several others assumed roles of wounded decoys. They stumbled slowly in opposite directions from families rearing young. Toughy, Shiny, and Smiley also distracted carnivores so that immature pikas might gain extra time toward preplanned escape routes. The decoy stood ready to bamboozle an enemy— and if necessary to die—while parents rushed their offspring to safety. Squawking like an outraged crested jay, counterfeiting a broken leg, limping, and pretending to fall frequently, Mama Sapiens and Limpy lured four-legged marauders along a well-practiced route not only away from colony babies, but also toward the decoy's tricky escape or my ammunition dump. Mopish and the hermit, apparently deploring any bent toward self-sacrifice, never participated in the decoy maneuvers.

In the suede softness of twilight, Skippy and the older females were first to notice any crunch of sand underfoot—a subtle simplicity that often escaped Toughy's and Shiny's attention. To all native wildlife, danger lurked most distinctly in contrasts.

Beyond the listless campfire shadows, an almost unbroken concert of owls chanted the mellowest of all wilderness notes. Inconceivable—but true—that these sweet-voiced phantoms on down-muffled wings could erupt into the most savage killers on Earth. The most gruesome fight I ever witnessed was between a fox and a great horned owl, in which the fox lost her life.

Certainly, not all night sounds reflected pleasure. Of an evening the canyon's most hypnotic atmosphere cloaked the highest profiles of danger, equally hostile to permanent residents and strangers. Lakeside coots betrayed their fear of darkness with broken-toned "sobs." Geese violated curfew to engage in high-volume family squabbles regardless of whom they disturbed. The great horned owl hooted torrid rage when lesser owls tried to dislodge him from their puny estates. Whoops of pain and terror rent the night when mink or marten slashed into huddling teal families, beaver lodges, or squirrel nests. It was especially after dark that the Square Top ecosystem became a drastic landscape steeped in danger—the devil's beauty.

The more those premature chills frosted the hardwoods, the earlier my friends tugged at the sleeping bag. Each morning's ratchetlike clacking of owl mandibles sounded closer. I often wondered how twelve to fifteen colonists swarmed down the rocky aisles, across the open lea, and into my forest campsite without casualty. On the now-bare meadow pika decoys seemed to play a daily presunrise game of baiting the raptors by darting and dodging back and forth to form crisscross, reticular patterns of dashing movement. Without exception they successfully grounded stooping owls with abrupt thumps, screams of rage and pain, and empty talons. Kowtowing to the Eagle Rock principle, I resisted an urge to break up those nerve-racking maneuvers.

Crouched on the lee side of the Ponder Rock on August 27, the same fifteen pikas and I listened to the metallic clicks of the pine sawyers that always preceded a dramatic red stage of the sunset. Atmospheric iron oxide dust acted like resin on the sawyers' mandibles and on the western sky like dye tinting. As a rule the fading light appeared visibly thicker when our region wallowed in sundown red. On the twenty-seventh we had just watched the gyrfalcon stoop and close with her archenemy, an arctic snowy owl. Both fell into a hazy ravine for a screaming orgy of sophisticated footing and beaking to establish dominance over the winter range. We turned our attention when a wren sang because obviously his heart was not in the song if he allowed the raptors' disturbance to compress and shorten his customarily abundant serenade. The pikas were not listening to beetles, raptors, or wrens. Infrasonic vibrations out of human range expressed more importance to them at the moment.

Except for thin, pearl gray ribbons of cirro-cumuli over the western minarets, the waning harvest moon promised an evening of lambent light. For half an hour Toughy and Mama Sapiens had been "eenking" for my attention. At length from the Lagomorph Creek trail, faint clinks of well-tempered horseshoes on stone reached my ears. By the time I had climbed down to the meadow, Eagle Rock had arrived, dismounted, tethered the borrowed mustang, and removed his gear. Enough dusklight remained to reveal hostility in his expression, inclemency he made no effort to conceal.

"And how goes the Emperor of Lilliput?" he asked without his usual smile. He did offer a strong handshake.

"Health of mind right now makes more sense than health of body," I said. "How about you?"

"Not good, Bob," the shaman said as he dragged his sleeping roll and *alforjas* (saddlebags) to the campsite. "Flare-up of the old pump. I haven't worked in a week."

"Sorry, Marc. Can I help in any way?"

"No. I had to find out how they fared in that goddamned wind." With a toss of his head he indicated the pikas. "I was afraid they'd lost half their garners."

"We've about recouped our losses. Carnivores keep me on the lookout more than wind. We've had an invasion since the storm. Worse than during the drought. Indigent bastards!"

"Where are any criminal carnivores, Bob? Only men have labeled them so. They never take more than they can eat. White men are the only overkill predators. How often have you heard the Little Chiefs quarrel with fate when the weasel wins?"

He spoke the truth, much as I hated to admit it. Carnivores engage in no blood baths, no poaching for profit, no pogroms. Starvation was wilderness enemy number one among carnivores and prey alike.

"I don't understand why your Earth Mother didn't give prey species one defensive weapon," I said more as a question than a statement.

"Whenever a weapon seemed reasonable, our mutual Mother tried it for a while during the last billion years. At one time doves and hares were armed." When I filled and lit his pipe, he asked, "How about a detailed account of that last windstorm?"

He praised my extra efforts. He even admitted that he

now accepted as a *fait accompli* my infrangible pact with the pikas—but not necessarily as fulfillment of obligation to Shoshone formula. Unbending as cragrock towers, he continued his saga of gloom from the armchair boulder behind the fire pit.

"You are now twenty-seven days into August. The Sagamore Council Moon is on the wane. You have reaped a few hard truths and some disenchantment, but I did observe some good-sized garners on the talus. Not enough, though. Are you still unwilling to allow them to work out their own destiny?"

"You are flogging a dead horse, Marc. What a helluva waste—what a heresy to allow the pikas to starve after all the bad luck they've been through! Where did I fail to do what I agreed to do at Sacajawea's grave?" I reached into my wallet and withdrew two fifty-dollar bills. "Here's a hundred dollars. Get a packer to bring in fives bales of alfalfa hay—just in case. Could I have done the job without establishing rapport with the Little Chiefs? And the answer is *hell no*, and you know it."

"For once you make sense. But I'll guarantee you they won't eat a bite of hay unless they are starving. It's not the solution. Didn't they find their own formulas to every problem for centuries before man arrived? Of course, you kept your agreement. My argument is that you *over*kept it. Your intimate relationship both with the Little Chiefs and with the bear has done the wild species harm in excess of the good of your contribution. I asked you here—would have come myself if it had been possible—on a one-time basis. There may be more to this year than meets the eye. Perhaps the Little Chiefs will point it out to you." He took the money and stuffed it into a saddlebag. "I brought steaks and baked potatoes and roasting ears. How's your coffee supply?"

"I still boil the grounds three times before burying them."

We prepared the meal and ate between arguments—an indulgent feast, each course of which we salted with nipping disagreement.

"You condemned me for pampering, yet you led the pikas to the marsh for *Datura.*" I thought I had him nailed.

"Aha! One occasion versus weeks of twelve-hour days!"

I also accused him of withholding information simply because he considered it privy to shamanism. To my surprise he agreed that each man had to learn and face raw truth in his own way in wilderness Eden.

"How much deeper the nights always seem over day, especially in the big of the moon," Eagle Rock remarked, as we lit our pipes and leaned back against the fireside boulder to enjoy glowing cones and the blue green fingers of flame that darted across the coals to create emberlight. "Only at night perspective creeps into the sky—eternity without circumference." He pointed out specific stars millions of light years beyond the Milky Way as orderly examples of elementary glimpses into forever. Slowly he unfastened a safety pin from a rip in his shirt sleeve and pinned up a hole in one knee of his jeans.

Marcos Eagle Rock was an intellectually complicated man, heedless of torn clothing but mindful of orderliness in the nighttime sky. No dealer in hand-me-down morality, he lived by Amerind code that has served human dignity, truth, and virtue for millennia; and though we disagreed on what was relevant, practical, or ecologically sound regarding my relationship with wildlife, we did agree without too many potshots at each other that brotherhood had to be the ultimate goal of civilized man. When I added, however, that working toward universal brotherhood with *all* creatures, not just the several societies of man, expressed the apex of human ideology, I discovered the one subject upon which we could finally agree without reservation.

"Unfortunately your words are like the night bird's song in the granite towers—an outback voice—with but four listening ears, yours and mine."

We relit our pipes and spat into the fire.

To shove my head onto the Shoshone chopping block at that critical moment, Tatters materialized out of nowhere—cocky and undisturbed. He stopped casually to study Eagle Rock's eyes, then mine. He walked directly to where I sat, turned around three or four times, and sidled up next to me. At that instant love, life, and governing intelligence were one and the same to the bear. The dying campfire cast a rosy yellow glow on the bark of surrounding pine boles. Eagle Rock glared at me in savage silence and conveyed optically—as he might to an animal—his unmistakable communication of disapproval. Instead of leaving when the shaman ordered him out of camp, Tatters raised his flews, bared his teeth, and growled.

"Isn't momentary importance to these creatures of some value—like *Datura?*"

"You exaggerate man's importance to them, Bob. They constitute their *own* importance. Hands off, man!"

"They have given me, and therefore man, a new perspective."

"A new corridor into human egotism. You've made some progress toward understanding their communications and needs. But what do you share with the *all-wild?* You don't share at all. You take. And that's where you and I nock arrows to our bowstrings."

"We met at Bird Woman's grave," I said. "I wasn't headed any place in particular. We talked. No big deal. It was a simple thing. I agreed to help your Little Chiefs in a short season, and that's what I've done even if I have tilted now and then with the sails of Quijote's mill—and your inflexible Shoshone principle. I've altered nothing in the *all-wild.*"

"But this is a year of *other* things, Bob. Brewing storms

you don't understand. You came up here and jousted with the truth. As I've said before, the Little Chiefs have withstood storms, cold, heat, floods, avalanches, epidemics, and predation since the first pair entered this canyon. I doubt they can withstand one white man—even a part-white man whose blood identifies with the all-Indian, a man who believes in Peter Pan instead of Gitche Manito."

Relentless Antagonists

"Please teach them to fear man before you leave— and, by God, that includes Tatters!" Eagle Rock said at sunrise as he counted and studied the little throng at our feet. He told me which pikas were missing. He looked me long in the eye when we shook hands. I thought he would never break the gaze. I would have died before looking away first. Without a final word or a glance backward, he mounted his horse and headed upstream toward Indian Pass. There is no equivalent of good-bye in Uto-Aztecan, the language of the Shoshone.

If the Square Top Mountain life force had a con- science, the Earth Mother had invested that faculty in Marcos Eagle Rock. In his judgment, sanity decreed that the wild remain *totally* wild. To mollify an encircling moral obligation, I resolved to teach the colony and the bear to fear me before I went down the trail; but my other side—

as in the case of the boondocks pudding—prevented the project from ever leaving the drawing board.

Tatters, the pikas, and I stood near the trail at a timberline flounce of juniper and watched until the shaman rode out of sight. I hoped he might look back and wave. But he didn't. Tatters, who was under injunction never to bother pikas under any circumstances, went to munch with spurious interest a nearby stubble of beemint and bunchgrass. Sensing impunity, the colony milled about the bear's feet, examining him much as the blind men examined the elephant. In my own mind I knew that Eagle Rock had ridden away wanting to say something he didn't say about that freakish year. Lest I appear overcurious about his cryptic meanings or concessive toward his more uncompromising side, I remained too reluctant to confront him about those "brewing storms" I didn't understand. At one point during the evening, he had conceded that brotherhood with all creatures constituted man's ultimate achievement; and that concession made me suspect he might have reappraised the extent of my design and labor. I know he was unduly suspicious of my notebook, into which I wrote most of what he said at the time he said it. He claimed I used shorthand so he could not check the accuracy of what I wrote.

Regardless of irreconcilable differences between us, at last I considered him a friendly antagonist. He brought ancient Amerind lore together with the finest fundamentals of modern ecology.

Marcos Eagle Rock! An all-man in the locution's grandest tradition. I may have overexalted him owing to the extent of my father-taught respect for Amerind mystique. Yet one minor episode really amazed me: the infernal fact that he *knew* without my telling him exactly which pikas had died in the interim between his last two visits! Naturally we designated them by different names, but I watched him call the roll with eyes that penetrated beneath every surface.

Eight lusty carnivores still hung around the canyon, poised to seize the first pika that relaxed vigilance. No orderly food pyramid prevailed, with chief meateater and prey at the top—no alpha, beta, gamma, delta that preyed upon the next lower positions. No true food chain arrangement flourished along the Green River tributaries. Excluding pikas, ordinarily timid nonpredaceous species stood ready to fight for the region's last edible herbs. Grazables, presumably the foundation of all food pyramids, had all but disappeared. Grotesque weather, flood, disease, or avalanche could wipe out overnight any level of delicate canyonland life. In addition to carnivores, competitors, and hardships of the land, the phantom guillotine, *time*, poised over every animal's head.

The shaman had succinctly outlined where I had profited more by the friendly association than the pikas or the bear in that they had enriched my life permanently and immeasurably. In return for a few hundred pounds of questionable hay or the pot scrapings, Tatters and the pikas had taught me a new approach to man-animal association. They were incapable of reciprocating for human affection, he had said, affection that would barely outlast the echo of my departing footsteps. In his words, my quixotic relationship "manifested the energy but not the wisdom to benefit their wildness."

The pikas' gentle exteriors masked an underlying ferocity for competence and determination beyond any of Eagle Rock's explanations. From an ingeniously executed sentry and decoy system to teamwork in harvesting and curing more than half a year's food supply, they demonstrated superb ability not merely to survive but to flourish. With no alpha personality to lead them, without totalitarian organization to hold families within the colony, they maintained stronger unity and order than any dominated, stratified communities I have known. Instead of wasting entire seasons and energy fighting for status positions, the pikas stored food and solved problems through co-ordinated brainwork, voice, teeth, and paws. They cooperated for the welfare and education of every youngster. Pika mothers and the likes of Mama Sapiens planned their "village" life with simplicity and mutual agreement. Predominance and preeminence had never won a foothold.

Over and over I wondered why Eagle Rock had decided they needed human assistance that year. There was something vital he had neglected to discuss. Most manmade "help" influencing natural communities has so far reflected a combination of effrontery and lunacy—often dishonesty. Between 1776 and 1976 more endangered native North American species have become extinct through excessive hunting, destruction of habitat, and mismanaged rangeland than have been saved by man's well-intentioned efforts.

Through the glittering Green River world those last days of August moved like a skyful of migrating swans—a sequential unison of whistles and wingbeats—and they were gone. Except for stripping elk moss from deadfalls, digging and cleaning a few tuberous roots, the pikas and I now gradually withdrew from harvest activities.

In spite of adversities and Eagle Rock's baleful predictions, we had kept our rendezvous with time.

Round-bellied colonists abandoned empty huckleberry brakes and indicated with upturned faces that I should follow them to windy shelves above the buckwheat flats. High up there on north-exposed flanks of boulders they gorged themselves on stippled crusts of black and orange lichens. As far as I have been able to determine, no substantial dietary reasons underlay their passion for "rock tripe," especially at that time of annual dormancy. To my own taste, lichen was less palatable than dry sponge.

Elusive as a dream, the first day of September dawned against a glacier-blue sky you could hardly find because of its transparency. Despite an unthawed updraft, eleven pikas led me down the trail to bogland at the mouth of the canyon. Tall, misty ground wraiths joined the biting breeze to dance first across the marsh and then to the leaf-less aldered banks of Lagomorph Creek. Cold and humid, the, foggy "ghosts" reeked of stinkhorn and death cup fungi as they fluttered in and out of the pine forest where they left their breath dripping from needle clusters.

Squawks from drowsy-faced loons gave voices to the dancing spirits. To evade the clammy ghosts while the pikas dug for sugar-heavy tubers, I sprawled on my belly, parting frostbitten marsh grasses, sedges, and mosses in search of tiny clenched fists of bracken fern still sweet and crisp. While I ate fern shoots, the pikas munched reed tubers and dormant strawberry stolons that tasted exactly like my rancid oleomargarine back at the campsite. They saved a few sweet tubers to carry back to their dens.

Scudding down the Porcupine Creek Trail and bel-lowing like a bulldogged steer, Tatters sprinted toward us, obviously only one jump ahead of big trouble. I lurched onto the path with my only weapon, a sturdy manzanita alpenstock. The bear's vagabond wanderings had launched him too often in conflict with an equally itinerant wolverine.

Sure enough, in hot pursuit flowed the sloe-eyed car-cajou, an ornery old varmint with guts enough to intimi-date any species in North America that would suffer his abominable conduct. This particular specimen wore a per-petual facewide "grin" that stretched into an infuriating death's-head every time he nipped Tatters's rear end.

With an insinuating smirk the wolverine snarled and lunged for the pikas as soon as the bear acquired what he misinterpreted as "safety" behind my back. Equally as flustered as Tatters, I swung the unbreakable manzanita with all my strength and landed a resounding whack across the attacker's shoulders. The wolverine fell, rolled back about five feet, but recovered instantly and prepared for revenge. Tatters reared, bellowed with a deep bass voice I didn't know he had, dropped his forepaws to his sides, claws out—the instinctive fighting stance of a grown bear. It was a stance the yearling had never dared use before. At that juncture I claimed my turn to hide. I jumped behind Tatters who now stood at least five feet tall. The wide-eyed pikas grumbled in dismay as they swarmed around my boots. Led by Mama Sapiens and Toughy, all eleven tried at the same time to climb my legs. Undaunted and maliciously savoring the writhing scene of panic in front of him, the wolverine hummed weird background

sound effects and crouched to spring. He had ample target. "Swat him, Tatters! Swat him!" I yelled.

Intuitively distinguishing between life-and-death pragmatism and a mere annoyance, the bear unleashed a right uppercut that lifted the charger four feet into the air. With a sequential left haymaker to the grinning head, he hammered the gargling wolverine back to earth. Without altering the volume of his snarl, the carcajou rolled with the punch, corkscrewed to his feet, and showered us with getaway musk and dust. I never saw him again.

On the way back to the meadow Tatters outgrew his yearling breeches. In those brief moments of truth he achieved the role of protector of man and pikas. He spent the rest of that day looking for other wolverines to clobber.

Two adult pikas—a male I called Pliny because of his insatiable curiosity, and a female referred to as Cocoa because of her color—descended the talus and met us at the meadow's edge. Both pikas indicated that something had gone wrong. I decided to climb the talus and search for lurking carnivores before conducting a personal-problem workshop on Meditation Tower. At muster on the rock I learned that Pliny's mate, Misty, was missing and that Cocoa was mourning a youngster—both probably waylaid while attempting to follow the rest of us to the marsh.

Almost as if each pika dreaded the monstrous law that all were born to die in hillside violence, the colony crept around me and stared through pleading eyes, probably begging me to reverse the direction of the wind. Unfortunately, they never modified that unjustifiable faith—a further vindication of Marcos Eagle Rock. The two bereaved pikas haunted my heels for days, screaming for a miracle to produce the lost ones. To tell it as it was, my eyes watered up every time I looked at Cocoa or Pliny. I didn't even try to communicate.

*   *   *

It may be that I got to know the pikas best after harvest responsibilities lay behind us. During those frigid September days, we practiced a welter of friendly maneuvers on the Ponder Rock, on tussocked downs, and on buckwheat flats where we hiked for exercise—wherever we happened to be—just for fun and to unprecedented companionship, without the pressures attending sickle, packrack, spread, cure, and garner.

If this account could end here on these satisfactory notes, I might indeed quit tilting at Quijote's goddamned windmill. But since I have taken an oath that my report covers the entire experience without fiction, addition, or subtraction (except certain anecdotes that might be considered incredible), I must relate with neither assuagement nor embellishment the final events exactly as they occurred.

Chaotic Realm of Truth

The fractious Tatters, who had discovered his machismo during the wolverine encounter, now muscled about as Number Three bull-o'-the-woods. Titan blood surged in his veins as he trundled up and down the trail, seemingly determined to avenge grudges against every form of life that had offended him during his tortured second year on Earth. Of course, he would steer clear of the grizzly bear, *Número Uno;* and the bull moose, Number Two; and maybe that crotchety old ram up on the phlox ledges that he could probably whip if he wanted to. He had no quarrel with the local cougar, who had always stepped out of the trail to let Tatters pass. But he now saw himself a stud to deal with. He had neatly unraveled a wolverine. Not everybody could boast of that.

Freed from the reins of caution and fear, he dashed toward the upper lake, determined to settle a backlog of accounts before hibernation. Clout—bone and muscle of the fittest in natural selection as formulated by Darwin, Huxley, and Lamarck: moral, ethical, and spiritual dogma governing wilderness justice. Coyotes had chased Tatters into the lower lake; a fox had once used the bear's belly for a trampoline when he had fallen asleep on his back; a bobcat had raked his claws across the yearling's fat fanny; jays, crows, and the whisky-jack had dive-bombed his ears; twice the antlered mule deer had almost impaled him just because he wanted to wrestle with a fawn. If he could only locate a specific smirky-faced wolverine, he would turn that "grin" inside out!

By noon the carefree woodsman had met none of his former tormentors. He pirated the decaying cougar kill from ravens and stoked his belly with overripe venison. Amazing how a full gut extinguished belligerence! Bruin fell asleep in tall cattails near the marsh where he may have dreamed about honey-smeared graham crackers and chocolate-coated peanut candy bars—his preferred decree of canonization for subjugating canyon dragons.

On the morning of September 3 a new psychological climate confronted me at the Ponder Rock—to which I sometimes referred in my notes as "Deliberationville." Shortly after sunrise that morning I saw a vixen fox drive a pika underground. At length the pika became impatient— precisely as the fox had reckoned—tried to emerge, and discovered too late that the calculating vixen had hidden so carefully between boulders that neither the pika sentries farther up the talus nor I had observed that the fissiped had not left. Limpy had uttered an "all clear" signal prematurely.

Gloomy granite towers to the west brooded under shadowless eaves of slate-colored nimbus. A grating monotone of pika cries—alarm signals—brought me to the assembly rock. I wondered why a delegation had not scurried to my camp with their problem. By then, of course, the vixen had escaped down the canyon with her breakfast, but the colony had reason to suspect vulpine trickery, and several adults indicated that they wanted me to man the ammunition dump should the vixen's dog fox show up.

I won't list the sources of monumental documentation available in good libraries everywhere, but many people have achieved varying degrees of intelligent mental exchange with domestic and wild animals. Yet for fear of ridicule, some have been reluctant to reveal the extent of their communication or the circumstances through which they accomplished it. Rather than set up a controlled investigation that could be repeated under scientific scrutiny—or summarily sabotaged by Marcos Eagle Rock—I experimented with the colony hopefully to achieve a few results similar to those reported by Amerind relatives as well as certain celebrated scientists. At the beginning of our association, Eagle Rock emphasized a thesis to which scientific observers have heartily subscribed: not everyone was attuned or adapted to maintain for a considerable length of time the level of intensive concentration necessary to establish mental relationships with another species.

At Square Top Mountain a tailor-made opportunity arose to determine whether a person could learn to communicate to *any* intelligent degree with animals. While knowledge might corrode the bright sheen of wonder, nothing could really dull the luster of truth. With drive, faith, time, and energy, the *right* person could duplicate my results with bears and pikas—perhaps with many mammals that had experienced no preconditioning brutality from man. As disclosed in my daily notes, a question often grated on my conscience: did I make bad use of human position—as accused by the Shoshone—or did I structure the experiment in ways unfavorable to the colony?

Frankly, I'm not sure.

At first the pikas were slow to make friends—sedulously choosy. They became companionable both on a one-to-one basis and as a community. Our common denominator for understanding, namely, *successfully communicated* trust, finally embraced a wide span of basic, primitive sensations far more subtle than elementary instincts.

The following incident illustrates for a *third* time a particularly engaging facet of pika mystery.

The pair I called Smiley and Bitsy had been among the first to accept my offer of friendship and trust. Bitsy's impish eyes often seemed to display a vivacious sense of humor that sparkled even behind her narrowed eyelid slits in the high-altitude sunlight. The couple lived in a terrace of boulders ninety yards above the meadow, and their well-constructed garners must have provoked envy throughout the hamlet. They had woven their hay above interconnecting corridors so that other pikas might eat from them when snow covered the slope.

About noon on that same day of the vixen fox, September 3, Smiley and Bitsy jumped from Meditation Tower and scurried to their bunker. Ten minutes later Smiley emerged, looked quickly about, then raced to a colony toilet fissure twenty yards across the talus in an area where there were no bunkers. No free-living lagomorph ever tolerated the squalor of a urine-smelly interior.

The secret of most carnivore success lay in the ability to strike before revealing any presence or hint of intention. The pikas often froze when a hawk or an owl flew over. Sometimes they ran in crisscross patterns to produce a confusing target; but on this occasion most colonists lay at siesta either on the windy tower with me or in their own bunkers. At the last moment Smiley may have recognized that the soaring gyrfalcon tercel was acting to seduce attention, while the falcon planed down at more than 100 miles an hour. When she closed with Smiley, I felt her talons in the pit of my stomach.

Eagle Rock knew what would happen as the result of my standing guard. The pikas had quickly reinvested unqualified trust, surrendering much of their own keen vigilance every time I sat with them—even after the day I fell asleep and two lost their lives. Although I offer no excuses, I had been neither lethargic nor negligent on this occasion—just caught off guard for a few seconds by two of Earth's fastest, craftiest birds.

Immediately after the falcon's close, most of the colonists sprang from rock to rock in a wild frenzy of shrieks and leaps. At length Bitsy bolted out to investigate the ruckus. When she whistled for Smiley, every pika fell silent. She sped to Meditation Tower. After scanning the slope, she looked me squarely in the eye. I turned away from her limpid gaze. She darted back to her den to see if Smiley had returned. Within moments she climbed slowly to a boulder crest and called ventriloquially across the talus. The truth probably came to her in segments—communicated through an absence of signals from the colony. During the next eighteen hours, strain mounted to so brittle a peak that no pika ventured either to the Ponder Rock or to my camp. Huddling near their doorways, entire families avoided all sound and movement.

Toward nightfall silence and cold crept hand in hand up the canyon. Not one cricket broke the stillness. Hoarse and weak, Bitsy alone continued to call. After the early dawn fox incident, our day had dragged out stark and hollow anyway. After the gyr, our curious and beautifully creative performances receded into memory like foggy details of a dream. Sunset's gentle tide swept away none of our justified gloom.

Lying on the sleeping bag within the flickering perimeter of glowing tamarack cones, I sensed the presence of Tatters, who in turn sensed something wrong with my evening mood. After studying my face for perhaps five minutes, he tiptoed away and disappeared into the night.

A truth always difficult to grasp was Eagle Rock's assurance that no carnivore ever prowled the talus for mischief. The wolverine pestered Tatters, hoping to evict him from the ecosystem in order to conserve the canyon food supply. Bears compete with wolverines for meat. No picaroons, no wanton destroyers existed among wild animals. But why Smiley? I kept asking myself. All life here bore the seal of mortgage from day of birth. A mystery of wilderness. Certain foreclosures came earlier than others. And there was no *why*.

Throughout the night Bitsy called. And even when her grief over insuperable loss dropped to barely a whisper, it still rasped my sleepless night. When I climbed the talus by flashlight at 2:00 A.M., many pikas stood at rigid attention on boulders above their dens. Bitsy dashed into her bunker when I tried to approach her.

Morning broke with delicate tints of green and yellow. After a quick breakfast with Tatters, I rushed to the frost-glazed Ponder Rock, but found myself alone with Mopish. The families clustered in their respective corridors. A mandate under the circumstances. Temerarius glared at me from behind one of his garners. He seemed to regard me as a dangerous stranger. It now seemed that Bitsy and Smiley were far more important to the colony than I had ever suspected. The pikas appeared to have resumed total wildness overnight.

From a boulder crest 200 feet below the tower, Bitsy crouched and wheezed with what strength remained in her lungs. She no longer called Smiley. By remaining in their bunkers, the other pikas indicated that they understood what man might never understand. In the chilling silence I watched her unremitting self-control as a weasel approached. I saw cold-blooded courage in her defiance of nature's first law, an indefinable dimension of the pika mind. She stood, not vacillating but swaying slightly as the weasel slowly climbed the talus. No facial expression betrayed any emotion, because she neither clenched her teeth, nor set her mouth, nor looked away.

With difficulty I overcame the reflex to intervene. It was no dereliction of anyone's vigilance that had brought about Smiley's death. No one could validly oppose her karmic right. My days of interference were over.

Suddenly Mopish leaped from the tower and disappeared beneath the boulders.

Unlike modern man, obsessed with horror at death in public, every colonist from within the labyrinthine corridors of the talus knew the time had come to emerge, cautiously to sit in silence, and watch. Through binoculars I observed a rare optical exchange between pika and weasel. Like a bartered pagan bride, Bitsy stood up to submit her body in fatalistic fascination as her proprietor slowly mounted the rock, reared, and faced her. He played his part as if he had practiced his role in advance. He was a spindling wedge of a weasel, as homeless as the wind, weak and emaciated from starvation.

I felt completely inadequate to the emotion, yet some force drew me imperatively to witness the spectacle for the record, regardless of personal involvement. Numbed and shocked, I stood quietly, gripped the field glasses, and waited. Frost from my breath accumulated on the metal parts of the binoculars.

There was no evidence that confusion clouded Bitsy's loyalty to her own best. No enigma was seen to twist her heart's will at the last moment. Perhaps she fixed the value of voluntary death as a time-tested victory of self-respect over pain and privation.

The pika and the weasel embraced with their forearms. Bitsy stood almost as tall as her emancipator when she offered him her throat. After one swift slash with razor-sharp incisors, his mouth closed over her jugular vein.

The last sound she heard above the weasel's eager

slurp drifted down from the solo of a hermit thrush on the buckwheat flats where we all had sat in the sun two days before. When the catchlights in her eyes went out and her arms fell limply to her sides, the weasel slackened his hold.

Two restless vultures circled slowly while the red-slobbering carnivore finished the liver. Thus, Bitsy, along with Cadger, Crusty, and Spot closed any controversy concerning lagomorph election of suicide.

Within a few hours the pikas had seen three members of their colony cease to be. Therefore, not wishing to intrude upon their privacy that day, I headed back to camp. Thickening cloud cover predicted more rain.

While climbing down the talus, I came upon Mopish. He sat eating from Smiley's and Bitsy's depositories. The vultures had barely gulped the pika's last shreds when the sluggard moved into the pair's vacant bunker. By shrieking and running circles around a large surface rock, the old faker tried to stop me with the disclosure of another loose boulder. I ignored him and returned to camp. Under the circumstances, the day was suitable only for bringing the notebook up to date.

Pillars of Water

Smothering black clouds extinguished the twilight. Not a pika had stirred since Bitsy's death.

You could safely bet that a storm impended when wet-smelling air delivered sagy essences from the foothills: basin sage, coyote mint, horehound, and pennyroyal. Another surefire sign our parched roughland would get an all-out gully washer appeared in lambency from friar's lanterns and foxfires over the mossy marshground at creekside—momentary glows attributed to spontaneous combustion of methane gas generated by mold fungus (*Armillaria*) during decomposition of plant litter. Prestorm conditions furnished the extra warmth, oxygen, and static electricity to ignite the tiny hydrocarbon pockets into momentary flares about the size of a lightning bug. For two days the vapor rings around the sun had made our air fuzzy and uncomely to see through, even when a breeze tugged its way up the canyon.

Shoshones never put much stock in white men's signs as predictors of rain. They barely glanced at the sky until thunderheads enshawled Mount Sacajawea on the Continental Divide. But deep inside, they always knew when to expect rain.

Still in the throes of emotional fatigue, I puttered around the campfire too upset to tinker with cooking other than to prepare a snack for Tatters. The smell of rain— brought about by the true sum of atmospheric conditions—bore down depressingly and unmistakably; so I pitched into several chores necessary to ensure minimum safety should the storm become violent. Camping *comfort* under stormy circumstances was patently nonexistent, no matter what precautions were taken.

Meanwhile, a layer of lumpy clouds sagged into the canyon and dumped a brief shower. Following the short rain, temporary cracks in the overcast admitted enough evening light to reveal peculiar activity on the bouldered slope. A thin veil of static electricity, rippling across the surfaces of wet granite, lured all pikas from their bunkers. Excited to abnormal hunger, thirst, energy, and excretion, they engaged in a wild round of out-of-season sexual activity. Through the binoculars I watched Mousey, Shiny and most younger colonists catapult from boulder to boulder as though a weasel were in hot pursuit. They had waged no similar frivolity before the harvest was stacked. Perhaps this levity helped them break through a web of grief and gloom.

Under a grumbling nimbus, the dusty hills below the lakes squatted as if bracing themselves against the seething sky's intimidation. Big bullbats—dark blurs against the low-slung clouds—flickered erratically up and down the canyon and shrilled to their kind to come feast upon a plethora of gnats, moths, and deerflies, swarming before the storm.

Now that golden-mantled ground squirrels, marmots, chipmunks, and most insects—overlayered with hibernation blubber or thick cocoons—had denned up until spring, chickarees piled three-foot stacks of green lodgepole cones without fear of raids on their pantries. They scorned and scolded me almost every other day when I tore their stacks apart, looking for stolen pika fodder, which they sometimes took and ate in spite of my vigilance.

Frenetic day-by-day glutting goaded Tatters as he invested endless hours toward accumulation of fat layers against the coming eight months when stringent scarcity and deep snow would keep bears in deep sleep. Aside from scattered whortleberry stands and the rare find of carrion, the Wind Rivers restricted a bear's food to larvae, frogs, mice, bulbs, tubers, and perennial grasses. To pacify his growling guts, Tatters resorted to aspen bark, assorted dry leaves, bones, feathers, bird nests, and deer manure!

As one last crowning effort to defy Eagle Rock's rigidity, I constructed a waterproof log lair and lined it with sphagnum moss. Tatters indicated that he understood when I showed him where he could "hibernate" in comfort and safety. By now he had grown a dense autumn pelage appropriately moisture-proofed for winter. He was in prime condition. The pikas also wore full winter coats.

Hawking a variety of husky-toned muttering and he-man swagger, the bear pigeon-toed into camp to impress me with his nerve to withstand the approaching storm. No amount of bluster, however, could dispel my suspicion that he fought off an urge to panic every time lightning jabs whittled the western minarets. Rejected by every native creature in the ecosystem (a painful insecurity when you come to think about it), he clung to my shirttail as his only social and kinetic reinforcement. Despite recent boldness of spirit, he suffered terrifying loneliness and discomfort. Like most bears, throughout his daily forage range he misbehaved sufficiently to incur hatred, resentment, fear, and revenge among permanent residents. Only the pikas were without reason to resent him. When he sometimes sat on the meadow and bawled from sheer loneliness, the cracking texture of his voice probably pictured the true image he contemplated of himself.

Friendly wildborn animals like Tatters and the pikas have taught us that many behavior patters as well as communication of essential thoughts require no vocal symbol. In warnings, for example, silent gestures are as direct and effective as voice itself, and often safer. For Tatters—and perhaps the pikas—the abstract, *fear*, when separated from a conviction of real danger, may have amounted to fringe pleasure. Real fear of danger (a hardier emotion)—like rage—required no vocalization to reveal the concept. This does not imply that pleasure, fear, rage, or hatred always arrived silently through animal eyes in the wild canyon.

Willing to gamble no more than minimum stakes during his courtship with calamity, the bear may have fidgeted with the notion that his recently acquired stealth and ferocity would enjoy permanent backup in the campfire man who always smoothed out his anxieties regardless of what badgered him. I prayed to all the gods, Earth Mother, Sacajawea, and spirits of departed Shoshones that Tatters would not require backup as a result of provoking the local grizzly!

Goaded further by imagination, I invited my pal to remain in camp that day in order for me to record detailed, accurate notes on his reactions during the storm's promised tympanic roar. Because of my paternal relationship, he felt no obligation to put up a sham front in my presence. He could be himself, square or fraud, and still get the attention he wanted—and needed. So he hunkered close beside me under the tarpaulin and shivered. All alone in deep wilderness, even a bear's machismo couldn't be expected to grapple with thunder and lightning. He stared in drop-jawed disbelief when I handed him a long-hoarded chocolate candy bar. The result of cubhood training, Tatters retained suspicious leanings, and I am sure he took it for granted that I was hatching some kind of sinister plot with that pencil and notebook if I was willing to underwrite my scheme with such a lavish price. Disregarding inherent mayhem arising from possible misunderstanding, I put an arm around his thick, woolly neck and nuzzled both sides of his face. He snuggled closer, dismissed suspicions that I harbored ulterior motives, and gurgled like a baby. He smacked his lips and licked his chops as long as the flavor of chocolate, caramel, and peanuts lingered in his mouth. Then he licked me across the nose.

When the tempest fell full upon the canyon, its precipitate fury and energy bombarded us both with fright. Faced at close quarters with unpredictable violence, I slowly remembered Tall Feather's comforting words: "Fear is a useless luxury. Your worst threat in the wilds is your own weakhearted self." Because of unintentionally communicated dread of impending danger, however, I failed to convey any comfort to the frightened bear, who quailed and moaned at every nearby electrical discharge.

Bending lodgepoles creaked and swayed like tortured specters in the tumult, but their graceful arms arched into the sky for welcome wetness. Chiseling bolts of lightning sculptured the cliff near the top of the talus. Then four successive explosions mutilated Eagle Rock's profile and flung the remnants crashing to the northwest ridge of the talus. Intermediate sheet lightning grounded itself in a jarring series of chain strikes as clouds seethed among the wet minarets to the west. The storm's debris continued to fall as talus builders, as it had fallen for millennia. In her extravagance, the Earth Mother built mountains only to destroy them.

During a tempest, distortion often displaces reason in the animal mind, including ours, and mischievous emotions engage in destruction worse than any storm's obstreperous onslaught.

Several gusts snapped my poncho back and forth with abrupt reports, like firecrackers, causing Tatters to bolt from camp and disappear among swirling columns of rain. Running after the fear-crazed bear—unable to overtake him—I was drenched to the skin in a matter of seconds in spite of the rubberized nylon slicker.

That which terrified a 250-pound bear simply amused the pikas. During the storm's fit and frenzy, its flashy electrical display illuminated a dozen dripping gale-blown colonists clinging to rockcrests, obviously reveling in the deluge. Thunderbolts irresistibly fascinated them. Each fiery clap brought heads and ears to outstretched attention. For such moments their heritage had psychologically textured them against discomfort, fear, pain, or worry; they apparently saw themselves as active participants in the tempest. For that reason they failed to brood over the hard prospect that the downpour could wipe out a substantial quarter of every exposed garner. Owing to a state of mental fatigue inflicted upon them by three shocking deaths a short time before the storm, they had neglected to transfer vulnerable stores into waterproof corridors beneath surface boulders.

Instinct coached most native animal populations during stormy weather. Knee-deep in the upper lake, a moose family slurped waterplant roots under squally conditions as if the moon were riding high. Disregarding the howling drencher, a small flock of bighorn sheep shuffled onto the denuded meadow and munched the spent stubble until a bull elk and his entourage horned them away. Families of deer stood at soaked attention in deep forest and never budged unless a cougar prowled. With equal verve, bob-cats, cougars, and waterfowl reveled in rain and, like pikas, exposed themselves in a mood of beatific madness. Upland birds and small mammals found crannied shelter along the range's western towers—or perished.

Unable to retrieve the bear, I sloshed back to camp, spread my soggy shirt, jacket, and jeans under the tarp, and crawled into the pup tent where my teeth chattered for an hour. In the acrid clutch of lightning ozone, the atmosphere rippled as if building up for an all-encompassing explosion. For a long time I lay gasping for oxygen and listening for combinations of sounds—signs that usually preceded slackening. Cliffhead thunder reverberated throughout the basin. Chatter from the gossipy creek, hiss of raindrops breaking into mist as they collided with pine needles, and always the wind's energetic bedlam blotted out any possible sounds that might have looked toward a breakup in the storm. How difficult it was to envision the volume of wind, water, and electricity a cloud could store!

At times I groped for faith that the Wind River Range, perpetually ravaged by elemental extremes, somehow paternally protected a majority of creatures within its citadel from nature's regular destruction. And again when faith waned during the tumultuous night, I struggled with an almost irrepressible urge to climb the talus. In vain I battled with the concept that the laws of evolution selected the survivors, that the mountains merely provided raw chemistry.

At daybreak rain still cascaded in recurrent torrents. With daylight, life slowly regained sanity despite the regularly spaced cloudbursts. One great fascination of rain lay in its mile-high columns that reached the ground as single drops except where plantlife shattered the fragile globes; and while the splashing of rain is a universally familiar sound, I had been unaware of the more subdued, lightly whistled music articulated by falling raindrops *before* they splashed against any surface. At 10,000 feet you can distinguish between *falling* and *splashing* raindrops.

Concern for the pikas finally drove me to recklessness. With gritting teeth and utter disregard for whatever ransom the storm might extort, I rushed from the tent, squeezed into my clammy clothing, grabbed a plastic sack containing the last pound of granola, and began a rash, impulsive climb. As I edged along in an agony of exposure, the drenched rocks became more slippery; my wrists throbbed from cold; icy rain coursed through my eyes and into my mouth; my sapless legs and arms barely responded to weakening commands to climb. Several boulders tilted, crunched, and slipped a little under my weight. I thought of Mopish.

Wringing wet and plainly exhausted, Toughy and Skippy followed me to Meditation Tower. Shiny and Bouncy stopped and waited for Mousey, Scotty, and two other pikas to join us. Mama Sapiens led two hardy youngsters through the downpour, but Limpy did not emerge. Temerarius left his bunker but refused to climb the rock; so, as usual, he forced me to deliver his share of the granola to his front door. All twelve pikas jerked their heads in unison as they followed the snappy trajectories of lightning stabs that streaked from the clouds' dark underbellies.

During magnificent storms like this, it may have been characteristic that among the pikas curiosity sometimes exceeded instinctive self-preservation, and if so, therein emerged intelligence with all its ramifications. They probably presumed that I had a strong reason for calling the muster. Mopish and three youngsters under his influence remained asleep in the dry bunker that had belonged to Bitsy and Smiley.

At length the downpour tapered off to drizzly showers, between which I passed out granola, affording those who came to the tower a ridiculous feast—a meal they devoured with gusto. Eagle Rock would have cursed the levity with unfiltered invective. After perceiving their enjoyment of the delectable breakfast, I was puzzled that the colonists revealed neither surprise nor dismay upon finding themselves once again facing starvation in the wake of the destruction sustained by most garners; but they communicated no concern. In a normal year most rainfall of consequence would have arrived *before* the beginning of intense harvest. In early July, cured garners were small enough to dismantle and carry into waterproof bunkers when heavy showers threatened. Also, if fodder got wet in early "summer," there was strength in the sun and wind to dry it before the ravages of mildew under endlessly cloudy skies. Dry snow, coming later, of course, would never damage cured provender. Among other things I didn't understand about that freakish year was the *volume* of untimely rainfall that poured over the talus.

At last the storm clouds receded, contentiously, it seemed, like a racking nightmare reluctant to let go. A herding wind milled the remaining nimbus into finials around the summits of the divide. Then the sun broke through to enhance the talus under one leg of a rainbow's misty span.

Still dripping wet and convulsing with cold, we sat irresponsibly in the teeth-chattering wind and stared at one another in wondrous amazement. Vividly colored light transformed each of us. We acted nakedly unaware—for the moment at least—of what tomorrow might bring.

To me each pika symbolized a pot of gold sitting under the foot of that memorable rainbow. In a breath the arc and our giddy dream dissolved.

There being nothing so tiring as idleness, we soon communicated the necessity for tearing apart every sodden, doughy garner in order to take advantage of desiccating wind and sun, but we paid tithe to the formidably hostile land. The storm had rendered one-fifth of the winter food supply irredeemable.

Until midafternoon the following day, we turned and redried fodder, all of which now smelled faintly of ferment and mold. Some shocks felt slimy as I lifted them to flat boulder tops. During a rest period on the Ponder Rock, ten pikas chanted. I marveled at their mettle. The better I knew them, the more they inspired admiration. Notwithstanding intense fatigue or distress, they still bounded for position near my face when we stretched out on the boulder.

Unfortunately, I thought, they had not resumed the all-wild state.

Owing to recent deaths on the talus, sentries shouted loud "eenks" if they suspected that any pika was sleeping during siesta; nor did any pika ever again depend upon my vigilance for warning them when a fissiped slunk toward Rockslideland. Predation figured as too high a price to pay for trust that failed. Delving into mysterious gazes, I often wondered during our intermissions at Deliberationville, whether they reflected upon departed friends and relatives. I cannot imagine their ever forgetting Smiley, Bitsy, Crusty, Spot, Drummer—even Cadger. At times their concentration appeared to be an act of recalling; they would sit for an hour, seemingly staring into the past.

Admitting that man as yet has but incomplete preparation with which to penetrate the thoughts of animals—even when they attempt to communicate with what we interpret as great effort—we do know beyond any doubt that they don't just sit there and vegetate.

On the morning of September 10, the pikas made no effort to conceal their agitation when they stole into camp before sunrise. Fully awake, I watched them approach the tent. Never ambiguous in disclosures concerning an urgent crisis, they all shrieked at once to indicate frightful emergency—after they made sure I was awake.

Frenzy in Troubled Eden

When the Earth Mother quarried the frost-riven west face of Square Top Mountain to build the dark-bouldered talus, she distributed her chips according to gravity. The brawniest Atlas at the bottom of the slope assumed the role of keystone. For hundreds of years that massive rock shouldered all detritus above it until intolerable tonnage and undermining water caused a general shift throughout the enormous masses of the scree. Such a rock had brought the pikas to my tent.

Toughy, Shiny, Mousey, and Mama Sapiens whisked ahead across the soggy meadow, glancing back every few bounds as if doubting that the rest of the colony and I were following. Out of breath after slushing through the mushy down, we arrived as a corps at the tired, fracturing mono-lith whose bulk resembled an oversized, inverted log cabin. More than half the boulder's mass now stood exposed, a consequence of erosion. With meadow soil over-grazed, saturated, and vulnerable—with moisture seeping down between ridges of the talus and collecting in the sandy loam around the base of the foundation stone—the great rock had begun slowly to creep in the direction of the sloping heath in order to unshoulder its overburden. Until the storms of recent years, gentle movement had allowed the bouldered hillside to loosen and settle gradually, without threat of landslide. But runoff from the last rainstorm had funneled toward the meadow, thus undercutting the principal keystone—the very foundation of the talus.

If the boulder suddenly heaved away, split, or sank into the unstable sog, a swath from the base of the Square Top cliff to the meadow—a surface area more than 300 yards long and 70 yards wide—would avalanche for more than an eighth of a mile, debouching a Niagara of boulders all the way across the open down and into the forest. Ridges of the talus would catapult to lower elevations, grinding to dust every living creature in their path. Under that specific 21,000-square-yard ramp dwelt the scattered pika families of Rockslideland.

At the height of the storm's towering fury sometime during the night, I distinctly heard a guttural roar and at the same time felt the Earth Mother's pounding fist. Rockslideland! Then it hit me square in the gutpit: that was what Eagle Rock called the talus. That word—Rockslideland—contained the hint to the information the shaman withheld. Landslide of rocks!

Trauma strangled the colony. A smothered silence permeated the jittery community while I struggled to assess the awful predicament. Obviously the pikas and their garners faced the necessity of immediate translocation, as foretold repeatedly by the sluggard Mopish when he ran from one loose boulder to another and clamored for my attention.

I could positively clock the big bulwark's jerky move-

ments. Furthermore, the condition now posed a risk too hazardous for me to chance my weight on the upper boulders in order to help move the animals and their winter food supplies. How was I to convey this message to the pikas? Almost in a state of shock, I stood trembling, unable to react. The whole talus seemed to be tottering. I began to look for a quick route to safety should the slide begin within the next few moments.

Exaggerating the calm and chill with its brilliance, the sun crept over the crystal crags of the divide. But the outward serenity at the talus masked an upheaval of foulest irony: the harvest had been gathered and cured before frost—stolen by squirrels, sheep, and wind; reclaimed, regarnered, or reharvested; damaged by rain and mildew; recured and garnered again. And now the abomination of impending landslide!

At first glance the predicament appeared hopeless. Impossible! To any reasoning person, one calamity on the heels of the next would seem to imply that no steps now undertaken could be effective. The talus was jinxed. I must have transmitted my consternation, because the pikas began an incessant shrilling like that of Aleutian petrels before a killer gale—a dark sound with fatal undertone, reflecting agitation distinctly offbeat from their usual whistles of alarm.

The animal sixth sense put the colony on an intense alert. While I stood and stared at the keystone, sentinels on the upper talus caterwauled the same distress signal over and over. Granting that I understood most of their calls, I had learned never to minimize any continuously repeated vocalizing. Many inflected nuances were too complicated for me to acquire during the time I worked with them; inflections, like optical messages, most often took too long for slow human reflexes to analyze. Like a fast-acting bullnettle, within a matter of moments this monstrous, pulsating shriek got under my skin, registering on my mind as a single voice.

Mama Sapiens and Toughy haunched on a nearby boulder and stared unblinkingly each time I turned my eyes toward them.

The immediate welfare of the colony figured uppermost in my commitment; and inasmuch as I had assumed that responsibility, drastic steps had to be undertaken within the next few minutes. Ridiculous. How could any single man confined within that time parentheses arrest and hold a slipping mountainside that an army couldn't stop? Of all possible years in the history of the talus, why should the calamity occur at that specific time? The thought kept recurring: Was that what Eagle Rock meant?

Although most people have never subscribed without reservation to claims for extrasensory perception, scientific thinkers have recorded abundant verification of the so-called sixth sense—insight, intuition, perception—showing that individuals have acted intelligently and without previous experience in circumstances with which they would normally be unable to cope. For centuries it went under the name of divine guidance. Without assigning the phenomenon to any category, mysterious or otherwise, somewhere in the fervor of the lilliputian mob—sustained by a unanimous sense of urgency, which they echoed without restriction—a temporary solution presented itself, almost as if the Earth Mother had shaken me and said, "Reinforce and block the keystone at once!"

If that boulder's forward and downward movement could be halted long enough to translocate the pikas and their garners to more stable quarters on a shelflike moorland adjoining the talus, we might trick the impending catastrophe into a permanent blessing. The stratagem offered the slimmest certainty of success, but it embodied the best thinking of which I was capable under that urgency. Not one minute remained to fritter away on vacillation. Within easy access lay two dozen 300-pound rocks. Gambling against a sprained back, I used a lodgepole log to lever every available impediment beneath the cornerstone's jittery keel. Rough surfaces engaged rough surfaces. When I grappled the tenth rock in place, the pikas' nerve-rasping shriek changed almost instantly to more wistful notes. For a reason that must remain unexplained, I suffered almost no fatigue during that unprecedented exertion.

I whistled the signal for silence in order to listen and feel for further slippage. What had been a moving scowl on the brow of the talus became, for the moment at least, a fixed frown. At length the pikas rushed jubilantly about, snatching and eating bits of dry grass, ricocheting off my shins, and chattering as if celebrating a reprieve. A strong suspicion smoldered in that part of my judgment where feeling and reason frequently hassled; celebration might be premature.

Reality, even in ostensible solutions of their problems, rarely justified my optimism for very long.

Slowly and carefully I continued to roll, carry, pile, or lever every rock I could move into the soggy pit in front of the Atlasstone. By four o'clock that afternoon my abject pessimism waned either from unwilling acknowledgment of fatigue or from wishful thinking. Movement of rock masses on the talus appeared to have ceased. I decided to climb to Meditation Tower for minute inspection.

What a terrifying experience, that shattery slope! My arms and legs twitched under goose pimples; chilly ripples raced up and down my spine each time I stepped on a loosened boulder that tilted under my weight and threatened to launch destruction throughout the talus. Many surface boulders had "floated" away from previously solid foundations. I could only speculate upon what had happened to the bunkers beneath that shaky, cracked eggshell.

Then I received an almost overwhelming shock.

Mopish and three young minions left the talus, waded across the soggy meadow, and scurried up the canyon trail. From a pigeonhole in his subconscious, the sluggard recalled the other pika colony that had visited our meadow earlier for exogamous swap. Two of the three youngsters now with him had been born in the other colony. Who can say that despair never played an effective part in pika life? Perhaps discouragement, the result of unappeasable odds against survival on the talus, had compelled the apostates to gamble for better luck elsewhere.

They had journeyed less than 100 yards along the trail when the gyrfalcon swooped and took the lagger. The falcon's kill was not as clean as usual, and the young pika's anguish echoed up and down the canyon for several minutes after the gyr had carried her victim out of sight. One by one, each of the four deserters fell into the talons of waiting raptors, and therein lay another hazard should I attempt to resettle the pika colony.

Cohesion in time of emergency distinguished the pikas. In this respect the group differed somewhat from assemblies of wolves, lions, sheep, elk, or simians. I never saw a member subjected to discipline, protocol, or forcible eviction; to my knowledge, no true show of leadership or pecking order ever emerged. And this made it appear likely that certain elements not generally recognized held the colony together. The same factors no doubt unite prairie dog towns, beaver lodges, and swallow communes, where a lack of rogues makes unnecessary almost any government, stratification, or chain of command. Indeed, in the course of observation it became clear that innate responsibility, a force stronger than family ties—more substantial than any known form of leadership—seemed to guarantee unity of the settlement. But this theory barely survived when four turncoats emigrated in the face of impending cataclysm. Family loyalty, suicide, and defection within the same province offered little to explain the adhering force of the colony.

While lying awake that night, awaiting doomsday for the remaining pikas, I seized upon what appeared at the time a sensible solution to the emergency. Owing to my feeling of insecurity toward conveying to the colonists "word" of the necessity for an immediate move, I resolved to seek outside help. Every alternative came back to the same person: Marcos Eagle Rock.

Late the next afternoon I arrived at Shoshone tribal headquarters in Fort Washakie, having found no one at Mrs. Howell's farm near Lander.

"I've got to find Marcos Eagle Rock," I said to a tribal official in the main office. "It's an emergency."

"Huh!" the man at the desk grunted. "You'll find Eagle Rock's ghost in the cemetery. He's dead a week or more. Heart attack, I heard."

"There's gotta be some mistake," I said, too stunned to make sense. "It hasn't been much more than a week since I saw him."

When the man shoved me a chair across the wooden floor, an avalanche rumbled inside my head.

"A week, maybe ten days ago. He'd been back in the boonies. Altitude must've got him, I guess. He was old. Only one family around here knew him very well. See the Howells over near Lander."

"I just came from there. Nobody home."

"Marc was a recluse. Somebody said he used to live here on the reservation—forty-odd years ago. He went away to college. Then taught school somewhere for about forty years. Spent his summers in the boonies up back of Pinedale. So we didn't get much chance to know the guy. He came here two or three times lately. I met him once. Hard to talk to. Old-time shaman. He had some kind of witchcraft hooey going on out at the cemetery. I heard that Mrs. Howell—that's his sister—is with a niece in Green River, but I don't know her address. That's about all I can tell you."

I explained what was happening at Square Top Mountain.

"Sorry. Nobody around here gonna help out with that. Right now everybody's sweating out late harvest after all that rain. Human mouths to feed when snow gets deep here in a month or so. We get some kookie propositions in this office, mister, but yours takes the feathers off the turkey!"

"I was hoping to get a wrangler and a train of pack-mules. I could stop that kingstone with twenty sacks of cement. I'll foot the bill."

"Try Mary Faler," he suggested. "She's got a pack outfit with mules near Pinedale. Better get a permit from the Forest Service first. You go pouring cement in the back country without a permit and they'll nail your hide to a barn door. Maybe you best forget the whole damned kaboodle."

"I'd like to do what Eagle Rock would have done. I can't talk to the Little Chiefs like he did."

We shook hands. "Drop in again some time." He was about to crack up with laughter.

"I'll see you."

Unable to get a permit to shore up the talus with cement, I didn't bother to see about mules.

"You're off your beam, Leslie." The ranger at the Pinedale Ranger Station refused to grant the permit. "Interferin' with nature in a wilderness area. We'd have them wild-eyed conservationists on our backs 'fore you left town. So skip it. No dice!"

I stocked up on assorted food staples, concocted five pounds of granola, and arrived back at Square Top Mountain late in the afternoon of September 12.

To my surprise, when I reached the marsh 250 yards below camp, Tatters ran down the trail to meet me. Since that flapping poncho incident the bear had acted as if I were angry with him. Apparently hoping my return might include a small jar of honey, graham crackers, peanuts, and another chocolate candy bar, he pigeonholed his suspicions, stood on his hind paws, and gurgled an extremely urgent message—a pretentious ploy, I thought, for such a scatterbrain. His garbled jargon made no sense until I saw an extremely timid cinnamon-colored two-year-old female bear on the far side of Lagomorph Creek. I followed Tatters to camp and presented him with some of the goodies he liked. He crouched for a time on the armchair rock while I hurried to check the blockstones. Returning to camp, I saw the two bears loping up the trail.

Almost at once I sensed a harrowing disturbance among the pikas. In fact, a climax of restlessness seemed to permeate all Cragrockland—nothing specific I could lay a

finger on, but an indefinable dimension of terror and skittishness pervaded. Somewhere in that general restlessness
was a part of Tatters's message, which I was unable to interpret, the part that had nothing to do with his newly acquired lady friend. The pikas swarmed down the talus and
met me at the Atlasrock as soon as they knew I had returned. I passed out two pounds of peanuts and molasses-
sweetened granola.

While they ate I studied with increasing anxiety the
block rocks and their effectiveness in checkmating the
restless movement. After taking measurements from the
four stobs I had pounded into the ground on two sides of
the keystone, I surrendered to gloom. Besides driving
many rocks out of sight into the wet soil, the huge lock-
stone had shoved its way about a foot toward the meadow
during my absence.

For more than 100 yards up the side of the talus the
seething tonnage leaned either directly or indirectly
against the one gigantic boulder. Pika country seemed to
be in a state of desperation. While I sat in a maddening effort to think, an osprey planed through the chilly air and
alighted on the Square Top crag where lightning had destroyed the old Shoshone's profile. The bird proceeded to
eat a large trout he had taloned in the lake. Outlandishly
enough, with the observation of the regal raptor's carrying
ability, a practical notion sprang into my head. I ran to
camp, then returned to the slope with a nylon rope and the
packframe. Slowly and carefully crawling over talus boulders, I finally reached the exposed garners that belonged to
Toughy and Skippy. In rigid silence and without batting
an eyelid, the colony sat around and watched while I tied
their provender to both uprights of the carrying rig. With
every outward appearance intended to portray urgency to
them, I shouldered the seventy-pound burden, toted the
precious cargo gingerly across the danger zone, and deposited it between two boulders on the teasel moorland adja-

cent to the talus, an area not affected by what might happen should the propstones fail to halt the forward movement of the keystone. The colony followed and haunched at my feet. Before returning to the slipzone for another garner—and praying for a miracle—I fell to my belly twenty-four inches in front of half a dozen of my closest friends and put everything I had learned into an attempt at an optical message.

The six displayed their usual affectionate attitude toward me; but their eyes now revealed hopelessness, uncertainty, and an inability to comprehend any communication I might endeavor to convey. I felt that once relocated in safe surroundings, they would again acquire the sunny expressions that had so beguiled me during radiant harvest days. For the rest of that windy afternoon I moved as many garners as possible. I worked for as long as I could see.

It impressed me as strange under the circumstances that woodland songsters congregated on the talus and sang at the top of their lungs while I worked. Whisky-jacks, crows, and grosbeaks, whose lyrics were about as destitute of melody as an old-fashioned cornshucking, stood on nearby rocks and matched troubadour volume if not musical quality. Local blue jays issued continuous warnings until the osprey glided back toward the lakes. It was particularly haunting the way that great raptor perched on the edge of the crag and carefully observed every move I made until darkness set in.

Sporadic wingbooms echoed throughout the canyon as grouse arrived from upper barrows and congregated for what looked to me like a squaw dance on the slushy meadow near the unstable keystone. Once they had mustered a flock of twenty—a contradiction of inherent grouse behavior—the birds darted single file, starry-eyed, and squawking down the trail as if they had lost the ability to fly. Ordinarily, grouse would rather starve than migrate from their native uplands.

Dimensions of Terror

Starlight luxuries to which I had become attached after enjoying daily sunsets with the pikas included reflective evenings with Tatters either on the trail during his forage or at the campfire. The infinite majesty of night itself with its own peculiar world of shadows, sounds, and smells provided a luxurious experience. Deep-lofted sleeping bag and the sensually rich enjoyment of total exhaustion just before falling asleep had afforded a material abundance that indulged my interpretation of delight.

On the evening of September 13 Tatters rushed to the campsite where I squatted preparing supper. He greeted me with a lusty two-paw whack and accepted but one graham cracker. He kicked up chunks of duff as he tore from camp and loped up the canyon trail to keep an important engagement with his new friend, who paced back and forth like a caged tiger while she was waiting for him. How he deserved to meet that one friendly animal—a perfect rewilding! I must have regained his full confidence, because he had dug dormant larvae without apprehension most of that day on the destitute meadow, nuzzling me on two occasions when I came down from the upper talus to check the mainstay. He gurgled like a cub when I put my arm around his neck and scratched his chin. With the encroachment of overcast, however, he may have foreseen the approach of another storm and that flapping poncho. I suspected a more natural reason for his hasty exit.

Half an hour before dark a single coyote, trotting across the meadow toward the lakes, stopped and stared fearfully for a few moments at the keystone. He sprinted away as if pursued—probably he had sniffed the man-smell on sweat-drenched boulders.

Thickening clouds again engulfed the canyon with a stuffed-in, claustrophobic seal. After total darkness had set in, twenty pikas from different boulders on the talus fifed such peculiarly fluted notes as might come from pipes of Pan—but not distress calls. Breathing inside the tent became more difficult and my thoughts included strangulation, smothering, entombment alive.

Quavering sounds—softened modulations of toads and dull-fiddling katydids and locusts—foretold a weathermaker. All that night the wind, forest, and distant thunder shouted competitive dialogue, just as they had done the time dry lightning crashed down and shattered Eagle Rock's profile. The combination of the coyote's unexplained fright, the menacing sky, the deep-voiced wind, the ceaselessly bleating pikas, and the reduced oxygen supply kept me on edge most of the night. None of the usual starlight luxuries were available to me.

By graylight the next morning, a norther had stripped the aspens to their buckskin bark of every lemon-yellow leaf. The cloud front had receded toward Yellowstone, but Red Desert dust veiled the sunrise. Needleblight frost had brown-coated the entire plant community. Eagle Rock and his pikas had read the signs correctly. An icy whirlwind now slashed across the meadow, then skipped to the rocky moorland to shake rime-twisted teasel, whose long stems drooped over the ramparts like fallen banners. I ran to the keystone. Each inspection had been more discouraging. The pikas remained silent, even after sunrise, and huddled somewhere out of sight on the talus. Maybe they had moved. I was betting my last chip on those translocated garners. On the way back to camp for breakfast, I recognized the acrid smell of blizzard on the wind. Cold, as such, presented no real hardship, but blizzard—and a threatening landslide!

Wispy vapors again seethed back and forth across the lakes like the elusive Saint Veronica veils that shunt about geysers in winter. Frostwoven dew had slimed the last soft-leafed annuals, withered the marsh-bred sumac and huckleberry, stripped every hardwood. You could follow the levels of rotting plantlife where encroaching frostlines each night had grayed more of the canyon.

I had barely reached the fire pit when the pika horde, stridently beeping, spilled suddenly down from the talus and scurried across the meadow. I rushed to meet them. They paced noisy figure eights throughout the campsite area, while I chucked rocks at a low-circling owl. The unstable talus nettled their minds. After bugling reedy-voiced greetings, with wide-mouthed, pert, gutty expressions, they circled in on the campfire rock and chittered. On that particular morning the pikas fixed their open-eyed stares upon my face without moving their gaze. Apart from signally few incidents, I had learned to read their early morning "bulletins" with a high degree of accuracy, perhaps through habit; but on this occasion only a distorted undercurrent of pressing emergency came through. Suddenly it hit me. Mama Sapiens was not with them to break the impasse! I was unable to locate Tatters or his cinnamon girl friend. Everything had gone haywire.

The pikas yelled as I had never heard them before. There was nothing to do but follow them to the talus. They not only expected it, they demanded it. As I clambered over sharp-edged rocks above the now-quiet keystone and struggled up the arched backbone of the talus, trying to keep up with the colonists, I realized that every anchor-stone on the slope had become unbonded. I don't recall climbing over one boulder that didn't rock, slip, or shudder a little as I rushed toward the upper levels. The higher I climbed the more dangerous the undertaking became. Footing now reminded me of the balancing acts of performing circus seals.

Colony tenements, corridors, dens, and bunkers were without question uninhabitable. Crunches and tremors at several elevations across the affected swath kettle-drummed a recurrent threat that avalanche impended, even though the keystone appeared to have stablilized. My reaction reflected not only basic fright but also recoil from the ugly face of an unconquerable foe.

It was also obvious that regardless of whatever physical means anyone might employ, human effort could amount to nothing more than temporary holding action— foxfire to a sunbeam. On one precarious perch clearly sensitive to the slightest movement, I stopped for a moment to regain wind. Long breath contrails rose on frigid updraft toward Square Top crags. Hoping for an intelligent option, I stepped from the rock in order to proceed to Meditation Tower.

A muffled squeak sounded far beneath my feet. The pikas had purposely drawn me to that particular boulder, had halted my advance and had lapsed into stony silence in order that I might hear that subterranean squeak. Before investigating, I automatically looked into the staring faces surrounding me and sensed their awareness that I comprehended at least part of the message. Two of my most loyal friends were missing: Mama Sapiens and Limpy. That thought had never left my mind from the time I had started to climb the talus. This incredible sequence further amplified Eagle Rock's tremendous intellectual achievement with his Little Chiefs. The trapped pikas had tried to find shelter during that frosty night. Their nook had caved in on them. The others came to me for help.

At the risk of finding myself pinned beneath two enormous boulders that teetered every time a gusty blast sneaked under them, I first rolled the largest rocks I could handle and anchored them beneath the two teetering monoliths. There was also the possibility of starting a landslide throughout that quarter of the talus simply by shifting the 500 pounds of weight.

Disregarding even basic good sense for the time, I clambered back down the talus and ran into camp for a long pole someone had cut at one time for a tent ridge. When I returned to the colonists, my heart was threatening to jump through my open mouth. I was convinced that not an erg of strength remained in my body. The pikas moved aside to allow me to slip the pole under the largest boulder and lever it into a safer position. With my sideknife and fingers slashing at dirt, gravel, and pulverized garners, it took less than ten minutes to rescue the venerable Mama Sapiens. An examination revealed no broken bones. While still cupped in my hands, she shook debris from her thick fur. I helped her remove grit from her eyes. Without the slightest margin for doubt, she communicated to me through hoarse squeaks and well-directed movements of her eyes that her protégé was still pinned under that big rock. With fingers now raw and bleeding from digging through dried thistle, gooseberry, and sweetbriar stems— the very stems I had helped the pikas harvest—I finally reached Limpy. He had grown into a supple and muscular young pika, but after his terrifying experience his body felt flaccid and lifeless. Resting in my right hand next to the warmth of a naked armpit, at length the little fellow struggled back to consciousness. He didn't move, even when his expression cleared, but he looked me straight in the eye and communicated his pain, the same appeal he had shown on the day I removed the thorn from his foot. Limpy reached completely across what I had regarded as an insuperable gulf between man and pika as he weakly extended toward me a broken front leg—then died.

At length regaining equilibrium by squelching my rebellion against the cutting edge of nature, I forced myself back to the task of relocating the pikas in order to prevent further tragedy. The one strength I could have turned to in those lonely hours of exasperation—Eagle Rock—was dead. Through simple logic I tried to deduce what he would have done. I cannot say for sure that he would have done *anything.* Landslides occurred naturally and interfered less with the Shoshone's grand principle than one presumptuous human harvester did.

The pikas had succumbed to a tragic epidemic of confidence—one of fresh and sassy faith in a primitive fixation that I could somehow reverse their ill winds. Mama Sapiens crouched nearby and stared at me as if she expected reanimation when I placed the dead Limpy where ravens could find his body. Toughy, Skippy, and eight others became suddenly noisy and eager for me to follow them. Although fearing to find other pikas also trapped, I seized advantage of their disposition at the moment to communicate with me. They shuttled back and forth more with exhilaration than with foreboding that might point to further tragedy.

Unexpectedly an ominous crunch grated above us. Rigid as if hypnotized and barely breathing, we listened for five minutes to the unseen giants that grumbled and chewed beneath the surface. That shaky housing project stood out as Eagle Rock's one mistake. In the shaman's mind, Gitche Manito had commissioned *him* the pikas' Saint Francis. He had calculated accurately every other difficulty, yet had proved himself cavalier in dismissing safe, empty moorland adjacent to the talus where he could have settled the colony years before Rockslideland reached critical imbalance. Rockslideland must have been his enchantment in years past—his dilemma, if in fact he recognized the existent problem. But the very name suggested a deeper meaning that he may have been hinting to me—an idea he may have wished to leave entirely up to me without interfering with my handling of it. I wish I knew!

For several minutes the whole talus rumbled and swayed like a vocano during an earthquake. Slowly silence and stability returned with a heavy settling into inactivity. I prayed that my conspicuous fright would communicate itself to the pikas.

When we reached Toughy's and Skippy's crumbling quarters, there stood their garners. Restacked, rewoven! It must have required many colonists' combined efforts throughout the night to carry and restack all the ricks I had removed to the moor. No wonder they shrieked all night! I climbed to Meditation Tower, suddenly vulnerable from within. Toughy and Skippy with all their peers followed and haunched around me in the chilly gusts. They chattered exclusively among themselves in a key barely audible to human ears.

I watched their eyes when a golden eagle soared from Square Top, stooped in midflight, and taloned the dead Limpy, whose body Mama Sapiens still guarded. She barely moved. Most eagles prefer to make their own kills. I quickly went to her, picked her up, and stuffed her inside my shirt next to my skin where she remained until she stopped shivering.

With a clattery crunch, an upper juggernaut half the

size of the keystone ponderously wheeled away from its mooring near the tower, crashed destructively with whirling speed and devastating force down the talus, and finally broke up. Quarter-ton pieces ricocheted to shuddering rest halfway across the meadow. Deep rumbling resumed. Expecting momentarily to experience an annihilating general landslide, I rushed the pikas to the base of the cliff, where we crouched near Temerarius's bunker. That the entire slope did not give way under that horrendous beating captivated my imagination. The awesome pounding appeared to have stabilized the talus. I coaxed most of the colonists to remain next to the cliff with Mama Sapiens while I carried the long pole down the north ridge to the keelrock. With that slender lodgepole shaft, I was finally able to lever heavy fragments of the newly broken boulder from the meadow to the front of the keystone. All movement stopped, including the mortar-and-pestle subsurface grinding of the giants.

With resumed determination to communicate the urgency of an immediate move, I ran to camp, shouldered the packrack, and climbed again to Toughy's and Skippy's garners. The pikas took up positions in a circle around me. I felt like the devil incarnate when once more I tore the woven ricks apart and carried the provisions to moorland safety. I worked most of that afternoon in the face of piercing voices and reproachful looks. It was impossible, of course, to do anything about those garners that colonists had stacked beneath surface boulders. At length Mama Sapiens joined us and sat alone, quietly studying what the other colonists may have interpreted as the meanest form of betrayal and piracy.

With locked-jaw determination, I seized the stores of Temerarius, Shiny, Bouncy, Mousey, and what remained of Smiley's and Bitsy's carefully stocked pantries. Between trips I coaxed the chattery, quarrelsome colony to big, loose, tottering boulders where I tried to convey the message as Mopish had done on so many occasions. I hated to see shattered the last vestiges of that manificent confidence and working rapport we had so laboriously built, but no alternative came to my rescue. Time had all but ticked away its course. Clouds seemed to threaten more rain within hours. A heavy downpour could either correct the tenuous imbalance and revert the talus to its former static state, or every foundation could collapse.

Mama Sapiens, my advocate on so many occasions, broke the deadlock between me and her furious tribe. Although I had seen no clear-cut manifestations of leadership, this one matriarch obviously inspired veneration, especially among the younger animals. On this occasion she muttered nothing, neither gestured nor beckoned; but the other pikas gradually grew silent and watched. She went to her own rock-damaged shocks, filled her mouth with silage wisps, and raced across the talus to the shelf-like moor where I had deposited all Main Street garners— and the stack that squirrels had rendered baneful.

For one not given to sentimentalism, I discovered a painful lump in my throat when at last every colony member began to transport fodder to the hillside moor. My Cherokee Gitche Manito soon saw my little votive fire of thanks that I kindled from twigs of lost garners.

By then it was late. Leaving further transportation of fodder to the pikas, I rushed to the moor and began construction of winter shelters, moss-thatched rock igloos with interconnecting corridors, deep chambers where huddling families could retain body heat when temperatures dropped to minus fifty on the Continental Divide— when pikas, gyrfalcons, and snowy owls were the only living animals near the surface of those frozen barrens. In front of the igloos I piled dry-stone fences to divert any formation of snowdrifts in 100-mile-an-hour gales. Each time a pika arrived with a mouthful of cured fodder, he or she approached the new quarters for a lively inspection.

All pain vanished from my cold and bleeding hands when Toughy and Skippy persuaded Shiny and Bouncy to inspect an igloo interior. Exhausted muscles found renewed strength and second wind. I felt that I could work for days and nights without respite.

At sunset four gunshot reports reverberated up and down the canyon, originating a mile upstream near the Granite Lake Trail.

Hunting season, Bridger National Forest!

Dusk was about to flood the canyon when two cackling flatlanders rode horses down the trail. A wrangler followed, leading seven packmules. Stretched over the paniers of the last two sumpters, two medium-sized bear skins rippled in the wind—one black, one cinnamon.

Tatters would never come back for the rest of his goodies that had meant so much to him. I would never get to know his one friendly canyonland associate besides myself.

What the conscience of man may dub *small* disasters among "lower" creatures are none the less disasters, whether occurring in the form of spectacles engendered by uncontrollable forces of nature or in the self-love of trophy exhibitionism sired by lingering Neanderthal genes.

The packtrain stopped at my campsite long enough for the wrangler to unload five bales of alfalfa hay. Overcome by a feeling of helplessness, I walked to the camp and prepared for the coming storm.

Tatters was no doubt easy prey for the riflemen. He would have stood up beside the trail, bawled, and waved his forearms, begging for a friendly handout or a chin scratching. Eagle Rock had never hurt him. Neither had I. Why should *any person*, therefore, do him harm? Trying to comprehend a deeper facet of the Eagle Rock principle, I compared the inestimable loss of my friend the shaman with that of my friend the bear. Without them I was in-

deed a poorer man. Both had enriched my life immeasurably.

Too mentally numbed by the shock of Tatters's need-
less slaughter to think clearly, and too restless to stay in
one place, I hiked to the upper lake. In the deathly prestorm quiet and darkness, the torturous loss really got to
me. No matter how I tried to change the subject of
thought, I relived every hour I had spent with the bear. His
funniest clowning and clumsy buffoonery now tore at my

heartstrings, and I wondered why I had ever laughed at his awkward efforts to impress the countryside with his maleness. Like the best of clowns, he never exhibited an analogue to the animal "smile" when he tried to be funny. I cursed the times I had been too tired to comply with his request to accompany him through the forest. He was the animal most eager to please me that I have ever known. He obeyed signals from my eyes as faithfully as the commands I sometimes uttered or showed by hand. Tatters

demonstrated his loyalty the day he stepped between me and the wolverine, the night he defied Eagle Rock in order to sit with me by the campfire. The bear and I had invested so many hours toward mutual understanding and affection that I could not believe that magnificent relationship was now dead.

That night has never ended.

Rain fell in torrents. Wind distorted every alarm from the talus. Boulders rumbled and tumbled from the slope and crashed onto the meadow with increasing frequency. Our Rockslideland world was indeed falling apart.

An Imponderable Void

Even during the storm's most dangerous pitch and rage, I sat under the tarp and brooded over the two bears' inexpiable end. The pikas now had safe, dry quarters—except that they went back to cling to the ancient boulder crests on the talus as was their pleasure during rainstorms. I could only hope they would return to the new igloos should the slope begin to slip during the storm. This new tempest rent the atmosphere with ominous odors. Throughout all preceding weather, the pungent fragrance of sage, mint, and ozone had stratified the air; but in the interim extensive black frosts had ravaged the canyon plantlife. The waterish wind now bore dank stenches of mildew and rot; there was no lightning to sterilize with ozone. Only cascades of torrential, lashing rain. That long night's vigil afforded ample time to deliberate upon my total experience with Tatters, upon Eagle Rock's prophetic words.

Under other circumstances, rain pattering on a tent's outer sweatfly or a taut-stretched tarp afforded the most soporific sounds imaginable, but on that night the din tormented every thought and precluded any will to sleep. The pup tent suffocated me with claustrophobia, so I sat on the armchair rock for hours and smoked up the last of my pipe tobacco. Shortly after the darkest period, possibly around 3:00 A.M., the rain and wind subsided. Low-hanging clouds still clamped a black velvet canopy over the canyon. Dripping trees and Lagomorph Creek continued to hiss. I could hear the continual roar of the Green River's glutted flood two miles away, pounding and clawing at sand and rocks in its channel. Sitting there with the sleeping bag wrapped around me, I had closed my eyes and had almost fallen asleep from sheer exhaustion after the last pika called. For a few moments I grappled numbly with a notion to spend the rest of the night inside the tent. Every animal must have been at rest, for no usual voices of night floated through the pitch-black stillness.

Then our silence crumbled.

With a sudden, extended fragmentation crash, the talus disintegrated. Echoes skidded explosively with equal din against every canyon wall, louder than thunder. Shock waves continued as loose boulders rained from the uppermost heights, as if dropped from massive clouds, long after the principal mass had plunged to the blighted meadow, obliterating what had been a flowering platform of life.

To overcome a seizure of shaking panic, I grabbed the flashlight and ran to the edge of the forest. Only half-conscious of what the consequences might be, I circled the buried meadow and tried with the flashlight's beam to fathom the black void where the talus had been. During that first deathly half hour following the landslide, I fought off an urge to rush above the devastation. Total darkness and intermittently plummeting boulders convinced me that nothing intelligent could be accomplished before daylight. Accordingly, I crawled into the tent with the sleeping bag to thaw out mental and physical numbness by means of the kinetic heat that claustrophobia generated. Cottony clouds sagged another 500 feet; their thickness seemed to bury the canyon and consume all its oxygen. Not a sound remained. Even the creek was now silent under that lid of pressure.

Lusterless orange dawn and a steady wind foretold rapid weather changes. In growing daylight I looked straight up a fifteen-foot wall where the staggering avalanche had rolled a morainelike dike. A hilly aggregate of mud and rock had miraculously stopped at the forest's edge, sixty feet from camp! The funneled juggernaut—the main talus ridge—had poured through a necklike narrows where the keystone had clung to the rocks I had rolled in front of it until crushing weight and flood water from above defeated the project. The extensive mass bore its own witness that no living creature could have survived the cascade of slush and granulating boulders.

For two hours I sat on the rock beneath the tarp and tossed wet pine cones onto the fire. The landslide having terminated my last excuse for remaining at Square Top Mountain, I finally began to pack my gear in order to break camp and head for home. One devastating thought fermented in my mind: I had not really communicated with the colony.

The pikas had followed eagerly to the teasel moor when Mama Sapiens finally transmitted my proposal, but they probably misunderstood the urgency of immediate dislodgment. Translocation had expressed an extravagantly wishful attempt, doomed before it began because the plan had crystallized too late to transport all garners and settle their owners in new bunkers before the crisis reached its breaking point. They no doubt returned to familiar ground that night to enjoy the storm on boulders under which they had been born.

Premature freeze now gripped the upper Wind River Range. In brilliant sunlight the new wind-hammered snow projected the divide as solid blocks of jagged ice. Total silence at an hour when most animals sang indicated that no life remained in the immediate vicinity.

Shortly before 9:00 A.M. a pika whistled.

I dropped my packing, grabbed the binoculars, and dashed around a tongue of the vast dike in order to climb a ridge leading to the teasel moorland.

Toughy, Skippy, Shiny, Bouncy, Tummy, and Temerarius crept down the ridge. On the other hand, about two dozen pikas, including the discerning Mama Sapiens, had probably crouched on or near Meditation Tower that night, reflecting upon the storm, when the precipitate landslip hurled them into eternity. I anticipated hostility when the six survivors reached me; but they simply walked slowly down the ridge and silently sat at my side. Together we surveyed with neither sound nor movement the frightful chasm left by the avalanche. No trace of antipathy marred their demeanor, only unfathomable anguish as their eyes adjusted to the shocking sight of what had been Rockslideland. Slowly advancing in evident pain, grievously wounded, the bedraggled little doe I called Peppy finally joined us. Before long I understood their message. They wanted me to rescue several that had escaped instant death. With binoculars I scanned the destruction. For a time intense fear kept me from entering the slide area. Then, hoping for a chance to reach trapped victims, I descended cautiously into the shaky ravine. But too many boulders still rocked back and forth in doughy ooze. Each step precipitated new slides and threats of further disaster. How often during the years that followed have I heard the lingering appeals of those impossible for me to reach in the rubble.

When at last the seven pikas realized that I could not recover their kin, they began the slow task of resettlement. Although a radiant way of life had collapsed into limbo, reacquired courage blossomed in an attack on fodder that lay strewn about the moor in soggy jumbles. An inestimable amount of winter provender had blown or washed away. What remained would not feed seven mouths for one month. But the five bales of hay—Eagle Rock's last service to his Little Chiefs—would see them through.

All our silage now emitted a soggy and fetid odor. The pikas went to work even before the wind rose to dry it. They followed me from stack to stack where we separated the compressed masses in order to prevent further mildew. During bright days after the storm, I worked feverishly to build stronger bunkers on solid ground. But their meadow now lay buried forever. I wondered whether the baled hay would merely tide the colony over until spring. Could they harvest sufficient forage from the barren heaths near their new homeland? If not, they would have to move again.

When the shapeless mass that now covered the meadow to an average depth of fifteen feet had drained to a degree that we could walk on it with comparative safety, the seven pikas and I searched among broken boulders for ricks of fodder that might have "floated" during the landslide. Every familiar talus landmark had shattered beyond recognition. We reclaimed less than ten pounds of cured provender from the slide area.

With further thatching and reinforcement to build into the pikas' new quarters, I decided to remain in Cragrockland until weather and starvation combined to drive me away. The pikas now huddled in their moorland shelters of a morning until I climbed the ridge. They never again came to my camp. For one reason, the detour around the slide was too great, the route extremely rough and broken. Seven small beings clung together in an agony of fear that would probably haunt them for the remainder of their lives.

Although the enigmatic little creatures had penetrated the innermost recesses of my consciousness, my understanding of pikas was destined to remain grievously incomplete. They left so many questions unanswered. Consider, for instance, the artful devices of Mopish as he leeched his livelihood—and then abandoned the colony just before the avalanche. If *he* expected a landslide, why didn't the others?

Had I been more perceptive, I would have recognized the subtle charisma invested in Mama Sapiens. I was too convinced that leadership was nonexistent in the colony. I know now—and suspected then—that I should have taken her on that stormy night to the solid headland east of the talus and sat out the storm with her. Had I done so, the entire colony would have followed and survived. I could have hired pack mules to haul in enough alfalfa hay and pellets to replace every garner.

It also occurred to me in retrospect that the pikas had depended upon the provender I harvested for them, or so I believed because Eagle Rock had convinced me. If indeed they suspected early frost, why didn't they harvest and cure their food accordingly? I learned later that the plant species they most wanted for curing were much too immature earlier. Without that extraordinary investment of faith in man, wouldn't Mama Sapiens or Toughy have translocated the colony when the keystone first began to creep? There were tantalizing questions that arose for months to come, with no answers ever.

A Silence in the Wind

On the morning of September 21 we worked high on the heath ridge, discarding rotten fodder and recovering the salvageable each time glacial wind blew it over the rim of the gully the landslide had created. While the fodder dried, I carried rocks further to reinforce the new bunkers and drift fences. I was about to begin the long, wearisome task of delivering the five bales of alfalfa hay when a delicate movement summoned my attention to the trail that wound along canyon contours below the slide area. An Amerind with long braids flapping in the wind walked toward the forest near my camp. He turned, shaded his eyes with a black stetson, and scanned what had been the talus. I picked up the binoculars. He was an old man, straight and agile, with a quick, determined step. As rapidly as safety permitted, I climbed down the steep ridge and shouted. The wind scrambled my voice against the Square

Top cliffhead. Although the trail across the meadow lay deep beneath landslide detritus, any passerby could easily proceed inside the level-floored forest around the massive perimeter of mud and boulders. After struggling through a thicket of thorny stuntbush and juniper, I reached the long-braided Amerind. He introduced himself as Larry Howell, long-time friend of Marcos Eagle Rock, brother-in-law of Marc's sister.

"I came up from the lakes," he said, turning his head to indicate his route. "I wanted to overtake you before you went to all that work to climb down the ridge. I don't move as fast as I used to."

"Why didn't you holler?"

"Shoshones don't believe in hollering."

We both smiled.

"I see Jim Hollister delivered your alfalfa."

"Yeah. The pikas' fodder was nearly all ruined."

My first impression of Larry Howell was one of profound interest. He was a real flesh-and-blood human being whom I enjoyed meeting. As we sat on the armchair rock near the fire pit and sipped stale coffee, I explained what had happened.

"Many people don't believe the living can get in touch with the dead," he said in a monotone, "but here lately I've dreamed a helluva lot about Marc. I was at Tribal Headquarters the other day. The agent told me about your visit. Shoshones often speak in *fours*. Little Chiefs, avalanches, big weather, and you. Otherwise I might never have suspected a slip. One helluva mess, huh?" He turned his head toward the landslide and zippered up his jacket. The wind spewed a frosty breath.

Shoshones exalt a conscious pride in that part of their creed that venerates the number *four*. Four equal petals on magic dogwood, four equal seasons in a year, four equal weeks in each lunar month, four equal sides to every per-

fect square. Conception, birth, maturity, death of everything, including thoughts. North, south, east, west.

"Cicadas don't sing in time of the Hunger Moons,
Bob," Larry said. "In a day or two you won't even have
drinking water. You gotta leave at once before snow
blocks your way—your car, I mean. The agent at Fort Washakie was very much concerned about your safety—as
well as about the Little Chiefs. He wouldn't admit it to you
when you were down there, but he called me in. That's
why I'm here."

My shortage of supplies had already made abun-
dantly clear the inevitability of leaving soon. Although
provisions had run low, I fabricated every possible device,
even extending my diet to cattail tubers, in order to post-
pone departure.

"Another thing," he continued, "before Marc died, he
told me all about your and his quarrels. He knew he was
dying. Shoshone shaman. You knew that. It was natural
for him to wigwag with wild animals. A lotta Shoshones
do. He could look into the next season. Marc saw something in pikas most people ignore. He thought a lot of you,
too. But he was a stingy old geezer with secrets that should
have been passed on to the tribe. I mean stingy with us—
Shoshones. He took to his grave many secrets Sacajawea
taught his parents. Maybe because he had no son. No apprentice to pass the secrets on to. Did he tell you those
things? He probably told you more than he told us. He
said white men would laugh at Indian eye talk. He may
never have said it to your face, but he finally accepted you
as an Indian. There'll be several of us old-timers working
on his sister's farm over the other side of Lander. We'd
think high of it if you'd stop in on your way home and tell
us everything you've learned from Marc and his Little
Chiefs. We especially want to know why seven pikas understood your communication—that was about a third of

the colony, wasn't it? We've got a tape recorder, if you don't mind. We think Marc might have wanted it that way. The tribe ought to have that information. Marc's health was poor lately and made him change his mind a lot. Wasn't himself. You did say all but seven were lost in the slip, didn't you?"

"All but seven," I repeated. "Yes, Marc was a man without vanity. He was neither indifferent nor shallow. Wildlife recognized him instantly as a friend. Sure, we quarreled a lot about the bear and the pikas, but God knows I respected that man. Just about everything he predicted turned out the way he said it would—except for the slip. He may have even hinted at that. Did he ever refer to the talus to any of you as Rockslideland?"

"Rockslideland? I never heard him speak of the talus as anything but Skyland. *Skyland*, home of the Little Chiefs. I never heard of any Rockslideland before."

"My Cree friends often speak about eye talk. Marc knew I'd learned a lot from the pikas and the bear. He may have thought that certain communication between humans and animals should remain secret and should belong exclusively to the Shoshone Nation. Of course I'll drop by Mrs. Howell's farm and tell you everything I've learned, including what I got from Marc."

Larry rambled on for almost an hour about Eagle Rock, but declined to answer specific questions that he reserved as intratribal privilege: Why did Marc remain "unknown" at Fort Washakie? Why were his relationships with other Shoshones of such a distant nature? As a shaman, why did he refuse to pass on the teachings of Sacajawea to his own people? Could Marcos Eagle Rock in fact communicate with wild animals? If so, to what extent? Beyond the Little Chief Speaker mandate of his parents, why were pikas so much more important to him than other animals in the alpine ecosystem? Since he often stated that "wildlings must remain their own problem solvers," was

there not a much deeper reason for the numerous times he
had "helped" the Little Chiefs even though he *said* he did
not believe in "interfering or changing anything at
Rockslideland?"

Suddenly Larry stood up, offered a strong, meaningful handshake, and walked toward the trail below the
landslip. I followed his long, swift stride to the marsh. He
had parked his truck near the lower lake. Before he left he
pointed to a buttermilk sky over Yellowstone. "Antelope
coming to water," he said. "Snow soon. I want to be on
paved road before it starts. You best do the same."

I had yearned for deeper scrutiny into Eagle Rock, to
get another Shoshone's appraisal of the shaman's dramatic
relationships with animals and his principle of laissez-
faire; but Larry Howell kept eyeing those approaching al-
tocumuli. He must have had a personal reason for oppos-
ing any speculation upon what Eagle Rock had refused to
discuss with his people.

Both Amerinds respected the Little Chief hares as the
principal inhabitants of America's highest altitudes—native dwellers in fragile ecosystems at the tops of pyramids
that help keep the total environment habitable for other
creatures. In other words, the two Shoshones—and as I
learned later, many others—had bona fide reasons to believe that even the slightest damage along the Continental
Divide could induce an unfavorable chain reaction all the
way to sea level, east and west. Both Shoshones were discreet, educated men. Both gently reminded me that white
men had already fumbled irreparably, not in malice but in
ignorance, with plant and animal species they had not intended to harm.

When the pikas called again, I climbed the ridge. For
the rest of that day I stretched out on the barren moor
away from the wind. The seven pikas huddled inside my

heavy down jacket next to my body for warmth, but not one of them dozed. At least two questions were finally answered. With or without an impending landslide—or Marc Eagle Rock—they would never have accepted my role had I not gotten to know them as intimately as I did. And I could never have finished the job without fulfilling my yearning to know them as I did.

After delivering the five bales of hay to the stone igloos on Thursday, September 24, I squandered the next two full days again on my belly in close contact with the seven. Our work together had ended. With the sweet alfalfa—which they relished instantly, in contradiction to what Marc had said—more than ample garners now towered on both sides of each bunker. I pointed to tight migratory wedges of snow geese: the season's last lofty formations from arctic tundra. There would be no more rain until spring. We studied at great length the northern horizon where thunderheaded stallions hurdled the frozen battlements of Absaroka, Teton, and Yellowstone. Withering up-currents watered our eyes. The northern Rockies now lay in the icy paralysis of winter.

On our last day together, as on the first, the pikas stood out in all their noble luster—not as lilliputians, not for man to measure in *any* dimension, not for man to compare in any way by the man standard. For me to remember of Square Top Mountain were the sunbeams, the moonbeams, and the smile beams; I had seen them all in pika eyes.

Temerarius, Tummy, and the crippled Peppy had woven their winter garners alongside the entrance to one of the new moorland bunkers. They would do their share to rebuild a colony according to natural laws millions of years operational before meddlesome man arrived. To be sure, it had taken a cataclysm to change the attitude of the hermit, Temerarius, toward his kind. At last he even communicated from a haunched position on my knee that I had earned his friendship.

Beginning about midnight on Sunday, September 27, big saucer-shaped snowflakes swirled and hissed earthward throughout the range. The swift-moving clouds did not appear exceptionally dense, but they dropped a foot of snow. Without a bite of food left, with my last match burned two days before, I shook off the dry powder that morning and crammed my gear into an empty rucksack. Eagle Rock's campfire pit, like the forest floor and the frozen Lagomorph Creek, lay deep beneath blue white drifts. When I shouldered the pack and slogged toward the buried trail, hurtling whirlwinds from a Square Top craghead wove stinging frost crystals from breath vapor onto my beard.

When seven tiny silhouettes clinging to snowcrested boulders on the moorland heights watched my hasty departure and whistled in chorus, I almost lost control.

It was a message. An invitation to return!

About the Author

ROBERT FRANKLIN LESLIE, of Scottish and Cherokee ancestry, was born in Texas in 1911. He has explored the wildest regions of the United States, Canada and Mexico, living for long periods of time in remote wilderness areas where he has associated closely with native wild animals of many kinds. He has canoed most western North American rivers and as a mountaineer has climbed many challenging peaks in North America, Europe and Asia.

Mr. Leslie received his B.A. degree from the University of California at Santa Barbara and his M.A. degree in botanical ecology from the University of Southern California. As ecologist and photographer, he has lectured widely and has appeared frequently on television and radio. He has conducted many photographic and adventure tours in North America, Japan and Europe. Fluent in four languages, he was a schoolteacher for many years before he started to write. Robert Franklin Leslie's books have been translated into many foreign languages and he is a frequent contributor of articles to national magazines. His home is in California.